Authentic Leadership– After God's Own Heart

Edited by:

John C. Reynolds, PhD
and Kurt Takamine, EdD

CONTENTS

ACKNOWLEDGEMENTS vi

FOREWARD x
Fred O. Walumbwa, PhD
William L. Gardner, DBA

INTRODUCTION 16
TRANSFORMATIONAL LEADERSHIP
John C. Reynolds, PhD

CHAPTER 1...31
EFFECTIVE GROUP DECISION-MAKING THROUGH
BALANCED PROCESSING
Mark S. Dickerson, PhD, JD

CHAPTER 2 59
MORAL LEADERSHIP:
Is Authentic Leadership a panacea for our leadership crisis?
John W. Washatka, EdD

CHAPTER 3 85
AUTHENTICITY AND TRANSPARENCY:
Is there ever such a thing as being *too* open?
Kurt Takamine, EdD

CHAPTER 4 .... **105**
SELF AWARENESS:
What are the benefits to "knowing thyself?"
Margaret Bailey, PhD

BIBLIOGRAPHY **132**

ACKNOWLEDGEMENTS

Authentic leaders are individuals that operate with a deep and abiding conviction of God's mission for their lives, and every participant in this manuscript was selected for their authenticity in their professional and personal lives.

All the contributing chapter writers (Mark Dickerson, John Washatka, and Maggie Bailey) embraced the task of communicating authentic leadership in a nontechnical yet accurate way. In their writings, they wrote from those places of balanced processing, moral leadership, transparency and self-awareness. That is clearly evident in their chapters.

Fred Walumbwa has been a wonderful supporter of this project, selflessly providing his time and expertise in dialoging about the field of authentic leadership, and in co-writing the preface for this book. William Gardner's contribution as the preface co-author was greatly appreciated, as both a scholar and luminary in this leadership field. We are indebted to both of these academics for their generative thinking in authentic leadership.

Books like this do not happen without the blood, sweat and tears of copy editors, project managers, and layout/graphic designer. In our case, all three were rolled into one person: Christina Zigler. It is because of her dedication that this book is currently in your hands or on your eReader. Thank you, Chris.

Nicole Spano and Calista Dawson did their magic with the graphic design of the front and back cover, and their efforts are greatly appreciated.

To Dawn McCool, Tami Heim, Carolyn Thompson and many others who are getting the books into the hands of our readers—Thank you.

We'd like to personally acknowledge our wives, Carole and Paula, who live out authentic leadership on a daily basis, and are constantly praying that we do the same. These women are the embodiment of patience and grace.

Most of all, this is an acknowledgement of all men and women everywhere that will engage Jesus' call to be real, and to "walk in the Light" (I John 1:7). May we all become authentic in our leadership responsibility.

JR & KT

Spring 2013

FOREWORD

William L. Gardner, DBA
and
Fred O. Walumbwa, PhD

William Gardner, DBA
Director, Institute for Leadership and Coordinator for the Area of Management, Texas Tech University

William (Bill) Gardner (Florida State University) is the Jerry S. Rawls chair in Leadership, director of the Institute for Leadership Research, and the coordinator for the Area of Management at Texas Tech University. Dr. Gardner's research focuses on leadership, ethics, and social influence processes within organizations. He has published scholarly articles in numerous outlets, including the Academy of Management Review, Academy of Management Journal, The Leadership Quarterly, and the Journal of Management. Extremely active in the Southern Management Association (SMA), Professor Gardner was inducted as an SMA Fellow in 2002 and served as the President from 2006-2007. In 2011, he received the Distinguished Doctoral Alumni Award from the College of Business at Florida State University.

Fred O. Walumbwa, PhD
*Associate Professor of Management,
Arizona State University*

Fred O. Walumbwa, PhD(University of Illinois at Urbana-Champaign), is an associate professor of Management at the W. P. Carey School of Business, Arizona State University. Dr. Walumbwa's main research focuses on positive forms of leadership including authentic, ethical, servant, and transformational leadership. He has published scholarly articles in a wide variety of journals, such as the Annual Review of Psychology, Journal of Applied Psychology, Personnel Psychology, Organizational Behavior and Human Decision Processes, Decision Sciences, Journal of Operations Management, Journal of Management, Journal of Organizational Behavior, and The Leadership Quarterly. Dr. Walumbwa serves as a senior research advisor for the Washington-based Gallup Organization. He is the series editor of the Monographs in Leadership and Management (MLM), Emerald Publishing Group, UK.

FOREWORD

Authentic Leadership—After God's Own Heart is a timely and relevant book. It explores value-based leadership behaviors that are essential for the effective functioning of every organization. We are honored to be called upon to write a foreword that briefly shares our unique experiences as authentic leadership researchers and explains why authentic leadership is critical for organizations (for profits, not-for-profit, government, military, etc.) and the challenges of today and beyond.

Let's start by asking a simple question: What is real in modern society? The challenges facing organizations including churches today are unprecedented. We all know of the high profile scandalous accounts involving business, educational, military, political, religious, and sports leaders around the globe that have seriously undermined trust in these institutions. Yet, people still want to identify with these institutions, even if they don't know how. In Christian organizations around the world, these challenges have led to confusion among followers as to what exactly it means to be a Christian, undermining their faith and causing many to feel lost. These challenges require a radically different brand of leaders and leadership—a value-based leadership perspective that emphasizes high standards of morality and ethical behavior.

Among the most prominent value-based leadership approach is authentic leadership. Authentic leaders are described as those who: 1) know themselves and are true to that self; 2) are guided by their core beliefs and values; 3) exemplify integrity and transparency; 4) engage in sound moral reasoning and honesty; 5) are good listeners that welcome both positive and negative feedback from others as a means of learning more about themselves; and 6) are courageous and passionate to make a difference without succumbing to any social influence or pressure. Such leaders are also described as being creative in their approach to the world and are self-aware of both their internal and external environment. A central premise of authentic leadership behavior is that such leadership requires an alignment between leaders' values and actions, and how they promote those values for the benefit of the larger community. This is why we believe authenticity in leadership matter most.

Make no mistake these are no ordinary behaviors as they involve high levels of real or perceived risks and costs on the part of the leader. However, because they reflect basic human strengths we contend authentic leader behaviors are exactly what we need to restore followers' trust in our institutions and leaders. Indeed, we have argued elsewhere that when leaders exhibit the behaviors described above they tend not only to create positive trusting relationships with followers, but more importantly, foster authenticity in others through role modeling. Preliminary research provides support for these arguments. For example, research conducted thus far regarding the consequences of authentic leadership suggest that leader authenticity and authenticity in general relates negatively to followers' burnout and positively to followers' empowerment, satisfaction, willingness to perform discretionary behaviors such as helping others, trust in leadership, commitment to the organization, work engagement, high self-esteem, overall happiness, positive psychological well-being, high work quality of relationships, and overall organizational performance. There is also some preliminary evidence suggesting that the behavior of authentic leaders can "trickle down" to their followers. In addition to the above, there are now programs, such as "Finding Your True North," which is offered through the Authentic Leadership Institute (ALI; www.authenticleadership.com), based on several years of practical experience and research, that are specifically dedicated to training and coaching leaders and their followers to be authentic.

Recognizing that authentic leadership is *not* a panacea for our leadership crisis, the editors and contributors of this book make very persuasive arguments that authentic leadership is nonetheless a key ingredient to solving many of the challenges that face our complex organizations and their leaders today. They do this by not only providing practical examples drawn from corporate, political, and religious spheres of life as well as their own personal life experiences, but also by tackling very tough questions on what it means to understand and be true to one's *real self.* We are also impressed by the personal reflections and applications provided after each chapter; indeed we find them to be very informative tools for helping readers to develop their own authenticity.

Over the last decade, we have been blessed with the opportunity to work with others to pioneer the theory, research, and development of *Authentic Leadership*—a concept that lies at the core of this book. We believe the editors and contributors have done an invaluable job of providing a powerful guide on how authentic leadership emerges, evolves, and develops over time. We wish you a good read and all the best in developing your true self and leading an authentic life.

Fred O. Walumbwa, PhD, Arizona State University
William L. Gardner, DBA, Texas Tech University

John C. Reynolds, PhD
Executive Vice President,
Azusa Pacific University
Chancellor/Chief Executive Officer,
Azusa Pacific Online University

John C. Reynolds, PhD, serves as executive vice president of Azusa Pacific University where oversight for administration and operations, financial and business affairs, legal affairs, information technology, university services, human resources, international initiatives, and leadership and organizational development fall within his span of care.

As chancellor/chief executive officer at Azusa Pacific Online University (APOU), Reynolds provides leadership for the administration of this virtual university and its strategic initiatives. Reynolds earned his undergraduate and graduate degrees in computer science and information systems in South Africa, and his PhD in Higher Education Leadership at Azusa Pacific University. He also serves as an adjunct professor teaching in his research interests of leadership, organizational effectiveness, change management, and strategic thinking.

In addition to his years of experience in higher education, Reynolds has worked as a strategy executive in the mining industry and as the global chief information officer (CIO) for World Vision International, a large private international relief organization (1991–2000). He is a regular speaker at national and international conferences throughout the world as a specialist in applied organizational effectiveness utilizing experience gained through his consulting, coaching, and counsel to non-governmental organization (NGO) leaders in more than 40 countries. Reynolds serves on several nonprofit and educational boards, including Christian Leadership Alliance (current chair), LCC International University (Lithuania), AP Educational Foundation (South Africa), and LCC International Fund (USA).

INTRODUCTION:
TRANSFORMATIONAL LEADERSHIP
John C. Reynolds, Ph.D.

Leadership is just not the same! Change, complexity, and compliance have become daily distractions from what we as leaders believe our real purpose and mission should be. Many ministry leaders today agree, and often lament, that the pace of ongoing dramatic change over the last few decades has cannibalized their time and is diluting their calling from God. If we think back just two or three decades when many of us were just starting to lead/manage people, we might reminisce about the simpler times when there was no email, internet, online giving, twitter, Facebook, iPhone, iPad, and the list goes on—leadership has indeed changed! Leaders are now expected to be collaborative with their followers, trustworthy, adaptable, dynamic change agents, and don't forget they must also produce results! Future leaders will be different — they will lead as agents of change focused on the call to lead from whom God wired them to be in a genuine relationship with their followers, those who choose to follow them.

Several years ago I was surprised and a little intrigued when our pastor introduced a new sermon series entitled, "The Three Kings." It was not a Christmas or Epiphany series, but was in fact a deeper understanding of how the character of leaders today, compared with the leadership style and behavior of three of the most famous kings in scripture: Saul, David, and Solomon.

As an organizational leader, and being a scholar of leadership, I was fascinated again by how uniquely different these leaders were, and yet how much we as leaders today could learn from each of their life stories. First there is Saul, leading from a position of title, focused on the power of being king, somewhat transformational in his leadership, and mostly faithful in his walk with God, but not always moral or ethical. Then there is Solomon, relying on his own wisdom leading with full confidence and dependence on his own knowledge and experience, often placing this wisdom before his dependence on God. And, lastly there is David, a man called to lead, genuinely concerned for his followers, failing often through his own humanity, but always returning to his Lord and God—really a leader after God's own heart.

Reflecting on the leadership of David and what I might personally learn and use as a leader in today's world, it was not a long stretch to characterize David as a leader who (1) knew who he was—he was obviously self-aware, (2) as a leader was fair and just—balancing his power as a leader, what needed to be accomplished as a leader, and the needs of his followers, (3) was mostly ethical and moral—that Bathsheba deal messed this one up, and (4) was definitely able to relate in a very transparent way with his followers—"He won over the hearts of all the men of Judah as though they were one man" (2 Samuel 19:14). David was a leader who today we might call a genuine leader: a leader who leads with congruence between his own personal identity, his strong relationship with God, and his actions as a leader. Contemporary leadership literature and theory might characterize David with these attributes as an authentic leader. As leadership theory develops we are beginning to recognize that leaders should have certain competencies such as vision, strategy, communication, and motivation, but also important is the recognition of their followers that they are authentic. This label of "Authentic Leader" transcends the transformational leader understanding to include the attributes of transparency, balance of power in the tension of title and process, doing what is right ethically, and showing genuine congruence between who the leader is, and how they behave. Let's explore what we mean when we use the term authentic leader in a little more detail in this chapter, with the outstanding chapters to follow that highlight application and experience in modeling authentic leadership.

Who is an Authentic Leader?

The Academic Perspective

Authentic leadership theory has developed as a unique leadership theory, evolving primarily from the field of positive psychology, which emphasizes positive emotions, character, and organizations[1]. This seminal focus on positive psychology has influenced the development of two significant fields of study in organizational science: (a) positive organizational behavior (POB) which loosely defined are the strengths and positive psychological capacities of the individual that can be measured and developed in an organization; and (b) authentic leadership. Influenced by the principles of transformational leadership, spiritualization, and charismatic leadership theory, an emerging and named organizational science of authentic leadership has emerged. Authentic leadership, originated more formally with research from the work of several social scientists, especially Fred Luthans, Bruce Avolio, Bill Gardner, and Fred Walumbwa. What has been of great value to the field has been their ability to measure and define the term authentic leadership "as a process that draws from both psychological capacities and a highly developed organizational context which results in both greater awareness and self-regulated positive behaviors on the part of leaders and associates, fostering positive development."[2] Followers might recognize leaders' authenticity a little differently as they identify leaders who are committed to their positive development in an organizational environment that encourages transparent and open decision making.

The Practitioner's Perspective

As my father used to quip, "you will know it when you see it." I wish there was a quick checklist, or a character "thermometer" that you could stick under a leader's tongue to measure their authenticity, but in my experience, it's a judgment call. Remember that being called authentic is **not** a label we create for ourselves, but is a subjective judgment made by others. You do not self-report that you are an authentic leader! Let me share a profile of one colleague (of many wonderful men and woman who influence my leadership) in my season serving in at a large international ministry. I actually worked twice for this organization, and on returning the second time, this leader was the only leader from the executive suite to "come down" to the bull pen to welcome me back and share how much value he saw in my new role this second time around. He was genuinely interested in who I was and knowing how God was calling me again to serve in the ministry. But this was absolutely consistent with who he was and what we knew of him as both a person and leader. His defaults were decisions and processes driven by his internal principles and values without ever being coerced or worn down by consensus. More often than not, he was the last one to speak in a meeting, normally to assimilate the conversation, or to ask stretching questions, often initiating further discussion and always a better result. No hidden agendas, a straight shooter, a strong student, and servant of God—a genuine leader who I find myself personally and subconsciously emulating; he "leaked" authenticity.

What then is Authenticity?

Authentic leadership emphasizes the human trait of authenticity that is historically rooted in the Greek philosophy "to thine own self be true." This principle of self-awareness is foundational to all definitions and constructs of authenticity, authentic leaders, and authentic leadership development. Modern humanistic psychologists, such as Maslow[3], have highlighted that self-aware or self-actualized persons are generally authentic; they tend to behave from a locus of "who they are" as individuals rather than succumbing to peer pressure or external expectations. A perspective of authenticity is identifiable in a leader through two key principles: (a) the individual's self-awareness and ability to self-regulate, and (b) the expression and congruence of that self-identity as appropriately expressed as they relate to others. Authenticity in a leader is really the emergence of self in their leadership behavior and style. A lack of alignment between the leader's self-awareness and regulation of self, and his or her ability to genuinely express and project that true self, might potentially lead the follower to question the leader's authenticity, and ultimately perceive the leader as inauthentic or not trustworthy. Who of us as leaders have ever felt motivated by following a leader that does not "walk the talk?"

A Personal Authentic Leadership Model

To recap, leaders are generally acknowledged as authentic when displaying consistency between words and deeds leading to positive outcomes. Goffee and Jones in their book, *Why should anyone be led by you?* characterize authentic leaders as being individually distinctive, while trusted and accepted in the organizational culture to the degree that they can be agents of radical sustainable change.[4] Successful organizational change requires authentic leadership!

Gardner, Avolio, Luthans, May, and Walumbwa propose a self-based model of authentic leader and follower that integrates these two key concepts of self-awareness and self-regulation. Positive results in a research study testing a theory-based measure of authentic leadership using five separate samples obtained internationally and in the United States confirmed the validity of a multidimensional model of authentic leadership. The beauty of this research was that it modified previous working definitions of authentic leadership which validated it as:

> …a pattern of leader behavior that draws upon and promotes both positive psychological capacities and a

positive ethical climate, to foster greater self-awareness, and internalized moral perspective, balanced processing of information, and relational transparency on the part of leaders working with followers, fostering positive self-development.[5]

This new definition formalized four specific components of authentic leadership:

- Balanced processing
- An internalized moral perspective
- Self-awareness, and
- Relational transparency

that provide a researched and valid framework for measuring the authenticity of a leader. This breakthrough of new learning mitigated the subjective nature of authenticity in the leader-follower relationship, to an objective level that we can use for our own leadership development. The remainder of this manuscript describes and expands on each of the four aspects with personal leadership insight, experience, and passion by four great people leaders. As an introduction to their contributions, allow me to provide a short description of each.

Balanced Processing

Balanced processing is the ability of the leader to participate in a leader-follower exchange utilizing a relatively unbiased filtering of information that reduces the exchange to be distorted by the leader's ego, exaggeration, emotion, and sometimes ignorance. Authentic leaders are self-regulated and strong in their self-identity, they lead teams by leaving their ego at the door; they do not "power up" or assert undue influence as a leader, but instead engage and provide a balanced and informed contribution to the discussion. Authentic leaders are not motivated by title or power, but by the self-assurance and confidence in who they are as individuals.

Internalized Moral Perspective

Internalized moral perspective reflects the behavior of leaders as exhibited by the identification and regulation of their own internal values, in contrast to the external pressures of society and organizational norms. Fred Walumbwa (the co-author of the foreword to this book) describes this aspect of authentic leadership as a convergence of two original components: internalized self-regulation of leaders and genuine behaviors.

Self-Awareness

Self-awareness is the understanding a leader derives from assimilating personal circumstances and context and how this new understanding of who they are influences his or her personal worldview. In the context of authentic leadership development, this process always involves an ongoing review of past successes and failures, specifically life-changing events or trigger moments. As leaders, we must be life-long learners constantly calibrating and actively reflecting about who we are.

Relational Transparency

Relational transparency refers to actions that displays or manifests the leader's authentic self to others. This genuine style of relating or communicating one's true thoughts and feelings promotes trust and wellbeing with followers. Relational transparency is neither inappropriate nor emotional, however, and wisdom/discernment on how transparent to be is a perennial question.

Together these four components describe the framework for who we aspire to be as authentic leaders, leaders who intentionally relate from deep personal values and convictions motivated by the genuine desire to build trust, credibility, and the respect of their followers.

We are, as leaders, living in a new day where our leadership is defined first by who we are, and then by our authentic relationship with our followers. We do not only have to satisfy our external stakeholders with outcomes and performance, but must equally quench the expectations of our followers searching for authentic leadership and community. Although not exhaustive, this comprehensive framework of balanced processing, internalized moral perspective, self-awareness, and relational transparency is a solid foundation to measure and calibrate our authenticity as leaders. We are leaders in a dynamic world requiring leadership that transcends the ordinary—our God and our organizations demand the extraordinary. Each of us are to live lives and lead with an unbending commitment to authenticity. We are called to be authentic leaders!

Personal Reflections and Applications

1. Reflect on who you are first as a person and then as a leader. Do you see congruence between who you know you are (as God knows), and how you execute your role as a leader?

2. When you consider your presence in meetings, would you consider your role a coach/facilitator to an outcome, or bringing consensus to your own desired outcome?

3. What personal leadership practices have you implemented to maximize transparency with your followers but still maintain boundaries of professionalism?

4. How do you resist the urge to "power up" in a team discussion? Have you considered asking your team to hold you accountable?

Team Reflections and Applications

1. Provide a copy or explanation of the four components of authentic leadership provided in this chapter to your leadership team and have them confidentially and anonymously rate your leadership on a scale of 1 to 5 (1=Not evident to 5=Models all the time). Reflect personally on the feedback and how you might develop your leadership style in response to the feedback.

2. In a team meeting have each member record privately, and in their opinion, when any of the four attributes are evident in a positive contribution (using +), or when observed negatively (using -). At the end of the meeting allow time for members to reflect on their

scoring of the meeting and where future meetings might be improved based on these observations.

3. Discuss with your team what constitutes an authentic meeting in your organizational culture and how they might hold each other accountable for constructively towards that authenticity in future meetings.

Endnotes

[1] Martin E.P. Seligman, *Learned Optimism*. (New York: Pocket, 1998).

[2] Fred Luthans and Bruce J. Avolio. (2003). "Authentic Leadership Development" in *Positive Organizational Scholarship*, eds. Kim S. Cameron, Jane E. Dutton, and Robert E. Quinn (San Francisco: Berrett-Koehler, 2003).

[3] Abraham H. Maslow, *Motivation and Personality* 3rd ed., (New York: Harper, 1968).

[4] Robert Goffee and Garreth Jones. *Why Should Anyone be Led by You? What it Takes to be an Authentic Leader*, (Boston: Harvard Press, 2006).

[5] Bruce Avolio, Fred Luthans, and Fred Walumbwa, *Authentic Leadership: Theory-Building for Veritable Sustained Performance*, Working paper. Gallup Leadership Institute, University of Nebraska-Lincoln, 2004.

Mark S. Dickerson, PhD, JD
Sr. Vice President and General Counsel of Azusa
Pacific University

Mark S. Dickerson has been practicing law since 1976 and has served in private practice, as general counsel for a multi-national corporation listed on the New York Stock Exchange and as a member of a crisis management team addressing the legal and financial issues facing a large faith-based organization prosecuted for fraud and involved in one of the largest charitable bankruptcy proceedings in U.S. history. Dr. Dickerson currently serves as Sr. Vice President and General Counsel of Azusa Pacific University. He received a B.S. in mathematics from Grand Canyon University, a J.D. from Harvard Law School, a M.A. in Theology from Fuller Theological Seminary, and both an M.A. and a PhD in Human and Organizational Systems from Fielding Graduate University. Dr. Dickerson teaches graduate courses in both organizational leadership and human resource management. He has authored and co-authored several articles on organizational leadership, management education and theology. Dr. Dickerson serves on the board of directors of Christian Leadership Alliance, a national organization that seeks to equip and unite leaders to transform the world for Christ. He enjoys hiking and reading and is active in his community. He and his wife Barbara have two children and reside in Azusa, California.

1

EFFECTIVE GROUP DECISION-MAKING THROUGH BALANCED PROCESSING
Mark S. Dickerson, PhD, JD

During my years of observing and serving with the leadership of faith-based institutions, it has been rare for me to find an organization that has established an effective decision-making process that takes advantage of the creativity and wisdom of a diverse group of senior leaders. In some institutions, decision-making at the top is truly a top-down affair with no meaningful input from others who have relevant insights or experience. Some of the leaders of these organizations populate their advisers with "yes men" and use their power and position to ruthlessly suppress any dissent from their pronouncements. Those who disagree may be demonized or marginalized as lacking in faith, not in tune with the leading of the Holy Spirit or just not a team player. Others govern with charisma and their followers are too charmed to ask questions or express disagreement. Conversely, there are leaders who are conflict averse and find it difficult to make the hard decisions. These leaders are often either too paralyzed to act or rely on the consensus of their advisers—essentially abdicating their leadership role.

The authentic leader does not fit into any of these models. She surrounds herself with independent thinkers with diverse perspectives and experiences and encourages them to share their insights into all key decisions. She is aware of the traps of her own biases and the social pressures that can distort group processing of issues and takes steps to avoid both of those pitfalls. Most importantly, she has a strong moral compass and is unwilling to compromise her principles.

The Positive Effects of Balanced Processing

Authentic leaders reconcile the tension between adaptability and an unwillingness to compromise principles by possessing a clear moral compass that does not allow deviation, and at the same time, integrates sufficient self-knowledge and a secure identity that enables them to understand their own limitations, engaging with and accepting different perspectives without becoming defensive. Other authors of this book will address the importance of high moral standards (Washatka, chapter 2) and self-awareness (Bailey, chapter 4), but here we will dwell on the leader's ability to objectively analyze all relevant data and to invite contrarian views that differ from their convictions.[1]

It is also important to note that the component of balanced or unbiased processing interacts with other components of authentic leadership to produce positive effects. When combined with other components of authentic leadership, balanced processing of information creates a virtuous cycle. For example, one group of researchers posit that "self-awareness and unbiased processing should lead to increased self-acceptance and environmental mastery.... self-awareness and unbiased processing should enhance one's personal growth through self-development."[2]

Similarly, when combined with transparency and the motivation to benefit others, balanced processing builds relational trust in the leader. May and colleagues noted that the process by which authentic leaders make ethical decisions includes fair consideration of followers' perspectives and "transparent evaluation of all relevant alternatives and the development of intentions to act authentically."[3] Where transparency in the process supports the perception of shared values and interests between leader and followers, identity-based trust can grow[4]. Transparency by authentic leaders and congruency between actions and beliefs leads to trust[5] and the interest of leaders in the well-being of their followers supports relational trust.[6]

Balancing Competing Points of View

Further, studies in organizational justice indicate that employees' perceptions of the fairness of decisions made are heavily influenced by whether they had an opportunity to voice their opinion prior to the decision being made[7] and whether they feel that they have been treated with respect and dignity in the process.[8] Scholars have theorized that individuals are concerned with procedural justice because they care about being valued members of the group.[9] One study found that if participants have the opportunity to participate in the decision-making process, they have higher levels of trust in authorities, a more positive evaluation of the neutrality of the process, and a greater sense of status recognition.[10]

Examples from the Corporate Sector

Before rehearsing some of the dynamics of balanced processing, it may be instructive to offer a few illustrations of business, political and community leaders who exhibited or failed to exhibit openness to diverse points of view. In the business arena, Bill George, the CEO of Medtronics and author of a book on authentic leadership, determined to reshape the board of directors of Medtronics with a diverse set of individuals "who would trust each other, contribute to a flow of ideas, and be willing to challenge what was presented to them" when he became chairman of the board.[11] Warren Bennis[12] also describes both Andrew Grove of Intel and Jim Burke of Johnson and Johnson as leaders who selected lieutenants who had the independence and intellect to disagree with the boss and insisted that they engage in constructive dissent.

Similarly, Bob Lintz (former general manager of the General Motors Parma, Ohio plant) found that inviting input and engaging in open communication built trust and strengthened employee buy-in—"I let them know that I didn't pretend to have all the answers. We had a complicated business, and getting them to listen to one another effectively and share their insights was the way we were going to prosper best....It was a process where the outcome would be something where they'd been involved, engaged, and empowered to help make the decisions happen."[13] Lintz even developed a joint decision-making process with his union and found that "Helping the union understand where we needed to go as an organization, what kind of goals we needed to have, and what kind of hurdles and barriers we were going to have to overcome to make these things happen was critical."[14]

Profiles of Political Leaders

Abraham Lincoln: The Epitome of Balanced Processing

A prime example of a political leader who sought and carefully reflected on competing points of view was Abraham Lincoln. In her bestselling biography of Lincoln, Doris Kearns Goodwin chooses as the focal point of her study Lincoln's selection of and relationship with his greatest political rivals as the leaders of the executive branch of government and his team of advisers.[15] Rather than tapping his campaign supporters for important government posts, Lincoln selected an assortment of politicians who had campaigned against Lincoln for the "nomination" William Henry Seward of New York, Salmon P. Chase of Ohio, and Edward Bates from Missouri, as well as former Whigs and Democrats Montgomery Blair, Gideon Welles, Norman Judd, and William Dayton.

Clearly, Lincoln was not looking for a group of advisers who shared his points of view. When asked why he would choose a cabinet full of his political opponents, Lincoln told the Chicago Tribune: "We needed the strongest men of the party in the Cabinet. We needed to hold our own people together. I had looked the party over and concluded that these were the very strongest men. Then I had no right to deprive the country of their services."[16]

Two critical issues during Lincoln's term of office, the Emancipation Proclamation, and plans for reconstruction of the South illustrate how he balanced competing positions but remained true to his principles. In his Annual Message to Congress on December 1, 1862, Lincoln acknowledged the diversity of opinions concerning slavery: "Some would perpetuate slavery; some would abolish it suddenly, and without compensation; some would abolish it gradually, and with compensation; some would remove the freed people from us, and some would retain them with us . . . ."[17]

Lincoln also acknowledged that he was motivated by two somewhat conflicting values. In correspondence with Horace Greeley, he expressed both his devotion to preserving the Union and his personal sentiment "that all men everywhere could be free."[18] Similarly, in a letter to Albert Hodges dated April 4, 1864, Lincoln articulates his conflicting values and obligations: "I am naturally anti-slavery. If slavery is not wrong, then nothing is wrong....And yet I have never understood that the Presidency conferred upon me an unrestricted right to act officially upon this judgment and feeling. It was in the oath I took that I would, to the best of my ability, preserve, protect and defend the constitution of the United States."[19]

In addition to debating the merits of the proposed proclamation with his cabinet, Lincoln sought an honest perspective on the Emancipation Proclamation from his fellow lawyer and judicial circuit-rider, Leonard Swett, and rehearsed both sides of the debate.[20] Goodwin reports that "so evenhanded was Lincoln's debate that Swett predicted to his wife, 'He will issue no proclamation emancipating negroes.'"[21]

Once committed, however, Lincoln would not be swayed from his course. Lincoln's counselors advised him that the Emancipation Proclamation would lead to his defeat in the 1864 election, but he persevered nonetheless. On August 23, 1864, he reflected on the prospects: "This morning, as for some days past, it seems exceedingly probable that this Administration will not be re-elected. Then it will be my duty to co-operate with the President elect, as to save the Union between the election and the inauguration; as he will have secured his election on such ground that he cannot possibly save it afterwards." His assistant, John Hay, remarked, "If the dumb cattle are not worthy of another term of Lincoln, then let the will of God be done and the murrain of McClellan fall on them."[22]

Speaking of the Emancipation Proclamation, Frederick Douglass, one of Lincoln's chief critics, stated that "Abraham Lincoln is not the man to reconsider, retract, and contradict words and purposes solemnly proclaimed over his official signature. …If he has taught us to confide in nothing else, he has taught us to confide in his word."[23]

Lincoln's attitude toward reconstruction was anathema to Radical Republicans in Congress who wanted the South "laid waste and made a desert."[24] They moved the Wade-Davis bill through Congress which would have required more than half of the prewar voters of a rebel state to pledge to support the Constitution before the state would be allowed to rejoin the Union and provided for punitive measures against Confederate military officers and officials. While the Radical Republicans helped elect Lincoln, he held fast to his dedication to preserving the Union. Lincoln responded to the legislation with a pocket veto. Shortly before he was assassinated, Lincoln provided the most eloquent articulation of his views on this subject in his Second Inaugural Address:

"With malice toward none, with charity for all; with firmness in the right as God gives us to see the right, let us strive on to finish the work we are in; to bind up the nations wounds; to care for him who shall have borne the battle, and for his widow, and his orphan—to do all which may achieve and cherish a just, and a lasting peace, among ourselves, and with all nations."[25]

Margaret Thatcher: The Antithesis of Balanced Processing

A political leader who sought to surround herself with like-minded advisors and ruthlessly suppressed dissent was former Prime Minister of the United Kingdom, Margaret Thatcher. Thatcher saw life in very polar terms—you either believed as she did or you were the enemy. She did not permit dissent or seek consensus. When many of her cabinet members were threatening to resign, Thatcher simply explained, "As Prime Minister I couldn't waste time having any internal arguments."[26] Her confrontational style was captured in this quote by David Howell: "[T]he Thatcher habit of turning the whole process into one constant upheaval, with constant polarization of every issue, even after events had clearly moved in the right direction anyway, prolonged the turmoil and minimized united support for change."[27] Gardner states: "She sought to control everything, rarely delegated authority, slept for four hours a night, and fixed her eyes on every detail during her waking hours. Her self-confidence slid easily into intolerance, inflexibility, and moralism. She was widely seen, even by supporters, as domineering, mean-spirited, divisive, and unheeding."[28]

John F. Kennedy, Jr.: Situational Balanced Processing

Of course, leaders are not always consistent in their behavior. For example, President John F. Kennedy, Jr. took advantage of advisors with diverse viewpoints in taking action on some situations and surrounded himself with like-minded friends and relatives with respect to other issues. One Presidential biographer notes that none of those close to Kennedy would urge him to take action on the issue of civil rights.[29] Kennedy gave little attention to civil rights during his days as a senator and congressman. Later it appears that he carefully addressed the issue based on whether or not his stand would gain him more votes than he lost. Beschloss observes that Kennedy "promised to use [his] 'immense moral authority' to give Negroes full equality. But after his narrow election (with ninety percent black support), he stepped back from that pledge."[30] "Soon after JFK took office, Roy Wilkens came to the Oval Office and asked him to honor his campaign commitments. Wilkens was shocked when Kennedy airily replied, 'Why don't you call Ted Sorenson? Write him a memo. We'll see what comes of it.'"[31] According to Halberstam, Kennedy saw the Freedom Riders through a lens of political opportunism as making trouble for him rather than through the lens of those who felt that the civil rights of blacks had been denied far too long.[32]

However, when faced with the potential of a nuclear crisis over the presence of Soviet nuclear missiles in Cuba, Kennedy's advisors vigorously debated multiple options.[33] Indeed Kennedy broadened his team of advisers by seeking advice from British ambassador Ormsby-Gore. Robert Kennedy describes one such session with these words: "There were sharp disagreements. Everyone was tense; some were already near exhaustion; all were weighed down with concern and worry...."[34] Historians rank Kennedy's handling of this crisis as his finest performance as president.

Dynamics of Balanced Processing

Merely surrounding herself with individuals who possess different perspectives, expertise and experience is not sufficient to insure sound decision-making by the authentic leader. She must develop an environment that encourages candid communication. In order to encourage participation by members of your team, Yukl[35] recommends that leaders:

1. Demonstrate appreciation for input.
2. Utilize input wherever possible and provide explanations where input is not implemented.
3. Avoid becoming defensive.

4. Identify ways to expand on ideas of subordinates.

5. Praise good suggestions.

6. Demonstrate active listening skills. Clarify communication and demonstrate that you value the speaker by paraphrasing what the speaker says and asking them to confirm whether it is correct and by taking notes on what is said.

Next, the leader must manage group dynamics to overcome group biases and achieve the positive benefits of participation. Franz[36] (2012) notes a number of common issues that impede effective group processing. One is the presence of power differentials within the group that suppress the participation of weaker members. Another is that most teams focus on common knowledge rather than pooling the unique information held by each member. In order to take advantage of the collective group knowledge, it is necessary for the leader to press each member to provide data to support their views on each alternative.

Pitfalls of Group Decision-Making

One of the distortions of group decision making analyzed in detail by Irving Janis is the phenomenon of groupthink where the group begins to claim its own moral superiority and view opponents as evil.[37] Janis demonstrates this phenomenon in discussing the dynamics of the Kennedy administration's thought processes leading to the failed invasion of the Bay of Pigs in Cuba and the Nixon administration cover-up of the burglary at the Watergate Hotel. Esser and Lindoerfer[38] also added NASA's disastrous decision to launch the Challenger to the list of examples. With groupthink those who disagree are demonized, data that supports dissenting views are rationalized away, the collection of information is biased toward the group's foregone conclusion, and alternatives are not fully considered.

Another issue in group decision-making processes is the phenomenon of group polarization. Group discussion often polarizes the tendencies of individuals in the group and leads to individuals to choose riskier courses of action than they were inclined toward before the interaction.[39]

Effective Group Processing Approaches

Structured interventions such as the nominal group technique, the Delphi technique or dialectical inquiry are all designed to avoid these pitfalls in group processing.[40] These techniques are designed to increase independent input from members, give equal weight to each member's participation, improve recall of pertinent information, and reduce power differentials. In the nominal group technique, for example, group members privately write down their recommendations then publicly state them. Members are allowed to ask questions to clarify the recommendations but not to criticize them. The group then rank orders the proposed alternatives to arrive at the preferred solution. The Delphi technique involves a series of surveys administered to experts who respond to open ended questions in writing. Participants are invited to comment on the initial set of proposed solutions and then the process is repeated.

In general, leaders should not influence others by providing their views at the beginning of the decision making process. Ideally, they should have separate groups look at the same issue independently and invite outside experts to challenge the tentative decision and question any assumptions made or appoint someone as the devil's advocate. The groups should generate multiple options, argue against each of the options and compare proposed solutions with historical examples.

Traps in Individual Decision-Making

In addition to developing effective group processes, the leader must still overcome a variety of challenges to her perception, recall, and interpretation of information. Balanced processing can be inhibited by the leader's own ego defense mechanisms and biases that distort her perception, recall and interpretation of the information. As Nobel Prize winning economist Herbert Simon contends, individual judgment is bounded in its rationality.[41] We often see what we expect to see, we are motivated to interpret our own behaviors as consistent and positive, and our interpretation of data is influenced by context. Bowlby observes:

"Every situation we meet with in life is construed in terms of the representational models we have of the world about us and of ourselves. Information reaching us through our sense organs is selected and interpreted in terms of those models, its significance for us and for those we care for is evaluated in terms of them, and plans of action conceived and executed with those models in mind. On how we interpret and evaluate each situation, moreover, turns also how we feel."[42]

Balancing Our Self-Concept

Our individual self-concept influences how we make sense of experiences and what we remember.[43] According to self-verification theory individuals are motivated to protect a positive self-definition and they will tend to construct a social reality that supports their self-image. For example, the leader may filter out information that makes the leader uncomfortable. As Gardner et al. note, those with fragile self-esteem engage ego defense mechanisms that distort information: "Such persons find it difficult to acknowledge personal shortcomings, such as lack of skill in an area, personal attributes that they deem undesirable, or certain negative emotions."[44]

Like Hans Christian Andersen's characters in the fairy tale "The Emperor's New Clothes,"[45] leaders can deny the obvious. Zerubavel quotes an observer of President Clinton's delivery of the State of the Union address during his impeachment trial and shortly after the Monica

Lewinsky scandal was made public: "[Having] the impeachment trial and the president's speech hours apart is like having an elephant in the room . . .It's huge, it's undeniable, yet people pretend it's not there."[46] Similarly, a member of the House Budget Committee comments on denial by George W. Bush's economic advisors in reporting on the state of the U.S. economy: "they all ignored the elephant in the room. They ignored the fact that [although] the president talk[ed] about getting the country back on the path to a balanced budget, he was the first president in recent history to inherit not only a balanced budget but a budget in surplus …."[47] Zerubavel discusses the roots of denial, including social norms regarding what we notice, our desire to avoid emotional pain, and efforts to suppress or restrict access to information by those in power. The social dynamics of denial are such that our silence is itself deemed undiscussable.

Decreasing Bias

Overcoming such limitations on rational decision making often involves intentional efforts to open oneself to other perspectives. Bennis[48] recommends that leaders routinely read newspapers, magazines, blogs and other material that articulate diverse points of view. As Plous notes, "many of the most effective debiasing techniques involve the consideration of alternative perspectives."[49]

In addition, an awareness of sources of bias can help people correct bias. Avolio and Wernsing[50] suggest feedback, reflection and mindfulness (self-observation) as practices that enable leaders to learn about their implicit leadership theories ("process leader self-awareness").

Finally, Bazerman[51] devotes a chapter of his book to techniques for improving decision making, but notes that our judgment biases are deeply embedded and attempts to change our habits will conflict with our self-images as excellent decision makers. One approach that holds promise is the use of cases and simulations to enable participants to develop generalizable insights. Another is to invite an outsider with experience in the issues at hand to provide their more objective views. A third is to utilize computer models applied to repeatable decision making scenarios (the computer model is better at integrating information and avoids inconsistent interpretations). Finally, Bazerman outlines a multi-step process designed by Kahneman and Tversky[52] to determine the extent to which our initial expectations of a situation should be adjusted.

My Leadership Bookshelf

Bruce J. Avolio and Fred Luthans (2006). *The high impact leader: Moments matter in accelerating authentic leadership development.* New York, McGraw-Hill. Avolio and Luthans share their process for developing authentic leaders, including tools for developing personal psychological capital and taking advantage of crucible moments to accelerate the process. One of the chapters is particularly relevant to balanced processing of information, addressing the dilemma of knowing when to adapt to a changing environment and when to maintain a constant course despite criticism and pressure from stakeholders. The authors describe how the leader's self-awareness and ability to self-regulate are critical in avoiding the pitfalls of limited mental models or becoming locked into escalating a self-defeating course of action.

Max H. Bazerman (2006). *Judgment in managerial decision making.* Hoboken, NJ, John Wiley and Sons. Bazerman is one of the leading scholars on decision-making processes. This book is based on solid behavioral research, but it is written for the lay reader. It covers the many ways in which our decision making is influenced by biases, shortcuts in thinking or limitations in our ability to absorb and process information. The book ends with a full chapter describing techniques for overcoming our biases and improving decision making.

Timothy M. Franz (2012). *Group dynamics and team interventions*. Chichester, UK, Wiley-Blackwell. This book combines the findings of academic research and practical applications in developing high performing teams. It includes sections on creativity and innovation, team evaluation, collaboration, group decision-making, leadership, and virtual teams, among others. Each chapter includes suggested team exercises and citations to additional resources.

William L. Gardner and Bruce J. Avolio, et al., Eds. (2005). *Authentic leadership theory and practice: Origins, effects and development.* Monographs in leadership and management. Oxford, Elsevier Ltd. Three of the leading scholars on authentic leadership collected and edited this volume of academic papers on the topic. Highlights of the papers include discussions of authentic leadership development, the implications of spiritual leadership theory, and an analysis of the moral component of authentic leadership.

Aneil K. Mishra and Karen E. Mishra (2013). *Becoming a trustworthy leader: Psychology and practice.* New York, Routledge. The authors describe the fundamentals of building (or rebuilding) trust and then discuss the application of the principles in a number of contexts—including trust within teams, trust in virtual organizations, trust in the midst of organizational change and trust in healthcare providers.

Personal Reflections and Applications:

Rate yourself on the following:

1. I make myself accessible to others (including those with different points of view).
2. I routinely read periodicals, newspapers, blogs and other materials with competing perspectives.
3. I make certain to include diverse perspectives in making key decisions.
4. I create a climate that encourages input from followers (transparency; trust; openness to listen).
5. I utilize the input from others wherever possible and provide explanations for significant decisions.
6. I admit my mistakes.
7. I solicit the input of others before providing my own thoughts.
8. I praise good suggestions.
9. I exercise active listening skills.
10. I avoid becoming defensive.
11. I engage in reflection and obtain feedback from trusted observers to maintain self-awareness.

Team Reflection and Application:

Assess your team's decision making process by having each member rate on a scale of 1–5 the extent to which each of these statements accurately describes the process.[53] (1=Never, 2=Rarely, 3=Sometimes, 4=Most of the Time, 5=Always)

1. All alternatives are considered.
2. All objectives are considered.
3. A comprehensive process for collecting information is employed.
4. Consequences of alternatives are thoroughly analyzed.
5. Bias is avoided in the evaluation of new information.

6.   Consequences are re-evaluated in light of new information.
7.   Careful planning for implementation of selected option.

Experiment with a structured brainstorming process[54]:
1.   Divide the group into small teams and introduce the problem statement.
2.   Instruct each individual to write down their ideas and then circulate the forms to another in their group. The readers are instructed to add three to four new ideas (including new ideas or ideas that build on other ideas).
3.   Have the entire group review all of the ideas, eliminating any duplicates and identifying any themes.

Experiment with a structured group decision-making process (nominal group technique)[55]:
1.   State the problem.
2.   Instruct members to write down their solutions.
3.   Ask all members to share their solutions publicly. Members of the group can clarify ideas by asking questions, but they cannot critique others' solutions.
4.   Group members vote silently to select the group's preferred solution.

Establish group norms for decision-making and participation goals (may want to utilize a group process observer)[56]. Consider:
1.   How should participation be encouraged?
2.   What should be done to brainstorm a comprehensive list of alternative solutions?
3.   How should decisions be made? Should it differ depending upon the importance of the decision? Should a structured technique be used? Should decisions be made by consensus? Should the leader (or anyone else) be able to veto the decision?

Endnotes

[1]William L.Gardner, and Bruce J. Avolio, et al., "Can You See the Real Me? A Self-Based Model of Authentic Leader and Follower Development," *Leadership Quarterly* 16(2005): 343-72.

[2]Remus Ilies, Frederick P. Morgeson, et al., "Authentic Leadership and Eudaemonic Well-Being: Understanding Leader-Follower Outcomes." *Leadership Quarterly* 16 (2005): 373-394, p. 376.

[3] Douglas May and Adrian Chan, et al., "Developing The Moral Component of Authentic Leadership," *Organizational Dynamics* 32 (2003): 247-260.

[4] Fred Luthans and Bruce J. Avolio (2003). Authentic Leadership Development, *Positive Organizational Scholarship* Kim S. Cameron, Jane E. Dutton and Robert E. Quinn, San Francisco: Berrett-Koehler (2003). Roy J. Lewicki, and Carolyn Wiethoff, et al., (2005) "What Is The Role Of Trust In Organizational Justice," *Handbook Of Organizational Justice,* eds. Jerald Greenberg and Jason A. Colquitt. Mahwah: Erlbaum, (2005): 247-270.

[5] Gardner, et al, 2005, pp. 365-66.

[6] Gareth R. Jones and Jennifer M. George, "The Experience and Evolution of Trust: Implications for Cooperation and Teamwork," *Academy of Management Review*, 23 (1998): 531-546.

[7] Ruth Kanfer, John Sawyer, et al., "Participation in Task Evaluation Procedures: The Effects of Influential Opinion Expression and Knowledge of Evaluation Criteria on Attitudes and Performance," *Social Justice Research,* 1(1987): 235-249.

[8] Joel Brockner and Phyllis Siegel (1996), "Understanding the Interaction Between Procedural and Distributive

Justice: The Role of Trust," *Trust in Organizations: Frontiers of Theory and Research*, eds. Roderick M. Kramer and Tom R. Tyler, Thousand Oaks: Sage (1996): 390-413. Tom R. Tyler and Peter Degoey (1996), "Trust in Organizational Authorities: The Influence of Motive Attributions on Willingness to Accept Decisions," *Trust in Organizations: Frontiers of Theory and Research,* eds. Roderick M. Kramer and Tom R. Tyler, Thousand Oaks: Sage (1996): 331-356.
[9] Allan E. Lind and Tom R. Tyler, *The Social Psychology of Procedural Justice*, (New York: Plenum, 1988).
[10] Tom R. Tyler and Steven L. Blader, *Cooperation in Groups: Procedural Justice, Social Identity, and Behavioral Engagement*, (Philadelphia: Psychology Press, 2000).
[11] Malcom Fraser, "Leading Beyond Self: An Interpretive Biographical Case Study of Ethical and Integral Leadership," *Human and Organizational Development*, Santa Barbara: Fielding Graduate University (2008): 164.
[12] Warren Bennis, (1999) Managing People Is Like Herding Cats, (Provo: Executive Excellence Publishing, 1999).
[13] Aneil Mishra and Karen E. Mishra, *Becoming a Trustworthy Leader: Psychology and Practice*, (New York: Routledge, 2013) 72.
[14] Mishra and Mishra, (2013) 73.
[15] Doris K. Goodwin, *Team of Rivals*, (New York: Simon and Schuster, 2006).
[16] Goodwin, 2006, p. 319.
[17] Ronald C. White, Jr., *A. Lincoln: A Biography.* (New York: Random House, 2009) 181.
[18] White, 2009, p. 151.
[19] White, 2009, p. 260.
[20] Michael Beschloss, *Presidential Courage* (New York: Simon and Schuster, 2007) 110.

[21] Goodwin, 2006, p. 510.

[22] Beschloss, 2007, p. 96.

[23] Goodwin, 2006, p. 483.

[24] Beschloss, 2007, p. 111.

[25] White, 2009, p. 277.

[26] Graham Little, *Strong Leadership: Thatcher, Reagan, and an Eminent Person*, (Melbourne: Oxford University Press, 1998) 72.

[27] Howard Gardner,(1995). *Leading Minds: An Anatomy of Leadership*, (New York:BasicBooks, 1995) 232.

[28] Gardner 1995, p. 238.

[29] Beschloss, 2007, p. 244.

[30] Beschloss, 2007, p. 235.

[31] Beschloss, 2007, p. 243.

[32] David Halberstam, *The Children*, (New York: Random House, 1998) 254.

[33] Graham Allison and Philip Zelikow, *Essence of Decision: Explaining the Cuban Missile Crisis,* (New York: Addison-Wesley Educational Publishers, 1999).

[34] Allison and Zelikow, 1999, p. 359.

[35] Gary Yukl, *Leadership in Organizations*, (Upper Saddle River: Pearson, 2012) 116-118.

[36] Timothy M. Franz, *Group Dynamics and Team Interventions*, (Chichester: Wiley-Blackwell, 2012).

[37] Irving L. Janis, *Groupthink: Psychological Studies of Policy Decisions and Fiascoes*, (Boston:Houghton Mifflin, 1982).

[38] James K. Esser and Joanne. S. Lindoerfer. "Groupthink and the Space Shuttle Challenger Accident: Toward a Quantitative Case Analysis." *Journal of Behavioral Decision Making*, 2 (1989): 167-177.

[39] Scott Plous, *The Psychology of Judgment and Decision Making*, (New York: McGraw-Hill, 1993).

[40] Franz, 2012.

[41] Herbert A. Simon, *Models of Man*, (New York: Wiley, 1957).

[42] John Bowlby, *Attachment and Loss*. (New York: Basic Books, 1980) 229.

[43] Daphna Oyserman "Self-concept and Identity," *Self and Social iIdentity*, Marilynn B. Brewer and Miles Hewstone, (Malden: Blackwell, 2004) 5-24.

[44] Gardner, et al, 2005, pp. 356.

[45] Hans C. Andersen, "The Emperor's New Clothes," *The Complete Fairy Tales and Stories*, (Garden City: Doubleday, 1974) 77-81.

[46] Eviatar Zerubavel, *The Elephant in the Room: Silence and Denial in Everyday Life*, (New York: Oxford University Press, 2006) 13.

[47] Zerubavel, 2006, p. 11.

[48] Bennis, 1999.

[49] Plous, 1993, p. 256.

[50] Bruce J. Avolio and Tara S. Wernsing, "Practicing Authentic Leadership," *Positive Psychology: Exploring the Best in People*, ed. Shane J. Lopez. Westport: Praeger, 4 (2008)147-165.

[51] Max H. Bazerman, (2006). *Judgment in managerial decision making*, (Hoboken: John Wiley and Sons, 2006).

[52] Daniel Kahneman and Amos Tversky, "Psychology of Preferences," *Scientific American* 246 (1982): 161-173.

[53] Adapted from Patricia J. Hollen, (1994). Psychometric Properties of Two Instruments to Measure Quality Decision Making, *Research in Nursing and Health*, 17, no. 2 (1994): 137-148.

[54] Adapted from Franz.

[55] Adapted from Franz.

[56] Adapted from Peter R. Scholtes, *The Team Handbook: How to Use Teams to Improve Quality*, (Madison: Joiner Associates 1988).

John W. Washatka, EdD
Director of Academic Affairs,
Azusa Pacific Online University

John W. Washatka, EdD, Azusa Pacific Online University's director of Academic Affairs, is responsible for leadership and administrative oversight of all academic programs and related curriculum development, oversight of all faculty, and course and program assessment.

Washatka earned an EdD from Regent University; an MA in Philosophy of Religion from Trinity Evangelical Divinity School; a BA in philosophy from Northeastern Illinois University; and a diploma in Bible and Theology from Moody Bible Institute.

Washatka has more than 15 years of experience in Christian higher education, consisting of teaching and administration in both traditional and nontraditional settings.

He has three grown children and resides in San Dimas, California, with his wife.

2

MORAL LEADERSHIP:
Is authentic leadership a panacea for our leadership crisis?
John Washatka, EdD

Let me cut to the chase and say now that authentic leadership is *not* the panacea for our leadership crisis. Many of us who think we face a crisis in leadership believe the causes are deep rooted, comprehensive, and complex. While the causes of the crisis defy easy solutions, authentic leadership acknowledges the importance of recognizing the need for leaders to abide by a sense of morality that embraces the entire person. Authentic leadership is broader in scope than abiding by a particular moral code, and so a comprehensive consideration of authentic leadership is beyond the scope of this chapter. What this chapter endeavors to do is consider how authentic leadership can address the seemingly poor moral development of select individuals in leadership positions.

No One is Immune

It doesn't take the reader long to recall more spectacular examples of moral failure sensationalized by the popular media including Enron/Arthur Andersen. Individuals involved in the Enron scandal include Kenneth Lay, Enron Chairman and CEO and Jeffrey Skilling, Enron CEO and COO, who were found guilty of multiple counts of insider trading, and securities and wire fraud. You may also recall business magnate Martha Stewart, who was found guilty of conspiracy, making false statements, and obstruction of justice as a result of a stock sale that occurred just prior to the value of the stock plummeting. While corporations and politics—President Bill Clinton, impeached for perjury and obstruction (linked with the Monica Lewinsky scandal) seem to make the most headlines, other disciplines including sports (major league baseball players Sammy Sosa and Mark McGwire, steroid use) religion (PTL founders Jim and Tammy Faye Bakker, fraud and bribery), and the military (CIA director and retired four-star general David Petraeus, extramarital affair) have had their share of public criticism.

Not Just Big Business

And it's not just major, multinational corporations or larger organizations that are susceptible to ethical lapses. Groups ranging from privately owned small or mid-sized businesses are also vulnerable to poor moral judgments. The common denominator among them is that all have individuals as part of the organization, and typically poor ethics are linked with poor leadership.

Comparing Authentic Leadership to Other Ethical Systems

Unlike other leadership theories, authentic leadership combines a rediscovered and rejuvenated ethical theory with an emphasis on the humanity of the workplace. Authentic leadership, with its moral foundation in virtue theory, recognizes individuals as moral agents who have roles to play in resolving ethical dilemmas in the workplace. Other theories include *relativist* and *conventionalist* theories which rely on rather arbitrary and changeable principles, *consequentialist* theories which rely on anticipated results, and *deontological* theories which rely on rules. The emphasis by virtue theory on character traits and the central role of moral agency is perhaps what distinguishes it from these other moral theories. It's not just leaders at the top who are expected to behave morally. All members of the group have a sphere of influence in which they operate and practice moral authority. What follows are a number of basic steps individuals within an organization can take to model authentic leadership and practice moral behavior.

Think with Virtue in Mind

First, think with virtue in mind. A characteristic of authentic leadership is the possession of a sense of virtue, or at least the ability to think and act virtuously. Authentic leaders are to be guided by virtues when it comes to deciding and responding to an ethical dilemma. This section is a consideration of the role of virtue in authentic leadership, and attempts to answer the question, "What does it mean to think virtuously?"

At the very least, a virtuous thinker recognizes common virtues as moral strengths that are, or should be, part of an individual's character. Varying lists of virtues have been proposed over the years; however, what is important to note is the idea that an authentic leader can appeal to a common list of virtues that can form the foundation for any moral behavior. Recent research[1] has identified six virtues as being universal and recognizable across cultures. They are wisdom, courage, justice, temperance, humanity, and transcendence. The commonality of those qualities that are recognized as being virtuous, as well as those qualities that are vices, can be easily illustrated.

The Bottom Line is Not the Bottom Line

An example of a virtue in action is Howard Behar, former president of Starbucks International, who practiced humanity through how he demonstrated concern for his people over and above profits. As he writes in his book the role and development of his employees was critical.[2]

Relatedly, Behar practices a principle of authentic leadership when he comments on a leader being true to herself and her values. The guiding compass for an authentic leader through good times and bad times is the determination to stay true to her values. Behar warns about the temptation of losing yourself because of fear, frustration, and failure. Fear and frustration can be offset by practicing the virtues of courage and patience, virtues being foundational to authentic leadership.

Vices and Virtues

As a warm up exercise in a business ethics class for adult learners, I would split the students into small groups and ask them to come up with a list of attributes they would like to see in a spouse. I wrote their answers on the board, and with each group I wrote less and less because of the amount of overlap between groups. The list typically included attributes we commonly categorize as virtues such as honesty, integrity, patience, strength, etc. After the last group gave their list, I would pause, review the complete list, and ask, "So, what are some characteristics not on this list?" It was interesting to watch the expressions on their faces change as one by one they would say characteristics commonly characterized as vices like lying, cheating, stealing, etc. They began to realize the commonality of virtues and vices.

As a follow up to the warm up exercise, I asked the same groups to list the characteristics of a good employee. Because of the warm up exercise, they were not surprised that they were able to come up with a common list. Lastly, I pointed out the commonality between the two lists, such that the attributes that make up a good spouse are also attributes that make up a good employee.

Part of the exercise was to have them understand that it doesn't take a moral philosopher with an advanced degree to realize the falseness of the expression "what is moral for you is not necessarily moral for me." The class came to this realization as they were able to come up with a list of attributes they all saw as good or virtuous. In addition, they realized that the list of virtues spanned the categories of roles, such that virtues are virtues regardless of the situation.

Doing *and* Thinking

A virtuous thinker also makes a connection between a decision and action, and sees the two as interrelated. Classical virtue theory sees the attainment of virtue through practice. Simplistically, individuals who are not virtuous become virtuous by practicing the virtue, or by behaving how they think they ought to act if they did possess the virtue. For example, even if I am by nature impatient, I can become patient by practicing patience, and acting how I think a patient person would act. It is difficult to overstate the connection between thought and action in the form of practice, since practice is the means by which the virtue becomes part of the person and eventually becomes instinctive and natural.

In the same way, an authentic leader models the virtues of leadership even if he has not yet mastered the virtues. The authentic leader realizes development and improvement comes only through practice.

In a comical way, the movie "Groundhog Day" (starring Bill Murray) illustrates the outcomes of practice. The main character came to the realization that simply reliving the experiences without reflection, was fruitless. It was only when he began to think about how to better himself that he is able to take advantage of the "do over." It is only when he comes to that realization and he courageously faces his shortcomings that he is able to move on. Similarly, the authentic leader will learn from his previous experiences in order to practice the virtues and improve his decision making ability.

Should Your People Follow Your Example?

Related to the idea of practice is the model a moral exemplar can provide. An individual can think of behaviors a virtuous person would practice, but it would also be helpful to observe and follow an example. When they were younger, my children asked me how to throw a baseball. Since my athletic ability is virtually non-existent, we watched instructional videos that showed examples of good baseball throwing. In the same way, to learn how to act virtuously, we observe virtuous people. You may recall the "What Would Jesus do?" (WWJD) bracelets, popular a few years ago. Essentially, the bracelets are asking the wearer to consider the example of Jesus as a moral exemplar when considering some sort of action. We are to do what we think Jesus would do in any given situation. In the same way, the apostle Paul volunteered to be a moral exemplar when he instructed the readers of I Corinthians to "imitate me" (I Cor. 4:16, NIV).

Authentic leadership involves more than just practice. It involves an altruistic approach which results in a compassionate regard for people. Goffee and Jones in their book *Why Should Anyone Be Led By You?*, state that one essential quality of authentic leaders is that they "empathize passionately—and realistically—with people, and they care intensely about the employees."[3]

Tony Hsieh former CEO of Zappos, the online shoe retailer, would do more than a billion dollars of sales over the years. Zappos has been recognized as one of the best companies to work for and Hsieh writes about it in his book titled, *Delivering Happiness: A Path to Profits, Passion, and Purpose*. His people followed him because of his espoused values such as: "creating fun and a little weirdness," "building open and honest relationships with communication," "being humble," and "sticking by your values."[4] Hsieh is a good example of an authentic leader who inspires loyal followers.

To summarize, the authentic leader as moral agent relies on the virtues for moral guidance. Virtues are seen as those qualities that, when practiced, develop excellence of character in an individual. Those striving to be authentic leaders would look to others as examples of moral behavior, and they would also consider what they themselves would do in a given situation if they wanted to act virtuously and altruistically.

Develop the Ability to Think Morally

Models of authentic leadership include the ability to make authentic decisions, and then act on them. Many of the decisions authentic leaders make are related to situations in which a moral dilemma was identified. It is incumbent upon the authentic leader to recognize those moral dilemmas and address them within an authentic leadership framework.[5] Authentic decision-making includes the idea of recognizing moral dilemmas as well as considering the intensity of the moral issues. It may be helpful to consider the role of moral reasoning with these ideas in mind.

Kohlberg: Moral Thinking Levels

Thinking morally, or moral reasoning, is the manner in which individuals think about moral dilemmas. Psychologist Lawrence Kohlberg[6] has suggested that individuals think at different cognitive levels, which seems intuitively true when I compare my young adult children to high school or even college-aged students. My children tend to think in more complex and developed ways. Researchers, using Kohlberg's work as a foundation, have suggested that in the same way people generally think at different levels, they also think morally at different levels, ranging from the most simple paradigms (selfish and self-serving) to the most complex paradigms (others centered and guided by moral principles, including the virtues). For example, someone considering a moral dilemma at the most simple level would solve the problem by answering the question, in the most self-serving way possible, "What's in it for me?" Someone who has developed beyond the self-serving stage would tend to follow rules when it comes to solving dilemmas.

Someone considering a moral dilemma at the most complex level would be guided by moral principles such as the virtues, wouldn't be driven by rules, and would strive to build consensus. [7] Ironically, in a culture where rule following is valued—the military—my senior enlisted petty officer cultivated a workgroup that operated on moral principles and he constantly worked to build consensus among its members. He didn't micromanage us, he treated us like adults, and he encouraged creative thinking when it came to problem solving.

Educational Levels and Moral Reasoning

What is perhaps the most intriguing finding by the researchers (informally dubbed the "Minnesota Group"[8]) is what they identified as the most important factor when it comes to developing an individual's level of moral reasoning. Their research looked at factors including age, gender, ethnicity, culture, and education. What they discovered is that the single most significant factor in the development of moral reasoning is level of education, such that those who completed higher levels of education tended to think at higher levels of moral reasoning. Other factors such as age, gender, ethnicity, and culture were not significant.

What appears to be crucial to the learning process are the skills of critical and analytical thinking and self-reflection as a student develops. For example, colleges that focus on indoctrination and ideology (e.g., certain conservative Bible colleges and institutes) do worse than Christian liberal arts universities that focus on "truth seeking" when it comes to developing the moral reasoning ability of their students.[9] The implication is that those whose moral reasoning improved, were able to think for themselves and to be critically self-reflective. Moral training can begin at an early age either through parents or through organizations such as churches, Boy or Girl Scouts, sports teams, or service organizations.

However, the self-reflection and self-identity central to authentic leadership is developed later in life as individuals develop and mature through their teen years and early adulthood, years commonly associated with college.

What is also interesting is that it is not so much the kind of education as it is the level. Students across majors develop at about the same rate, and students within the major develop at about the same rate. Generally speaking, undergraduate college students think at a higher level than high school graduates, and graduate students have more developed moral reasoning abilities than undergraduate college students. Not surprisingly, terminal degreed and post-doctoral students consistently have the highest developed moral reasoning abilities.

Does "Knowing" Imply "Doing?"

What the research is **not** saying, is that those with a higher education are more moral than those without. Being moral is more than the ability to reason morally. While the research indicates a direct correlation between formal education and the ability to reason morally, learning or knowing the moral action to take does not make the individual more likely to take the action. Socrates' notion of "to know the good is to do the good" implies a relationship between knowledge and motivation, such that knowing the right action is motivation to do the right action. His notion does not explain individuals with advanced degrees who are corrupt. Knowing the good does not mean doing the good. While knowledge of the good can motivate an individual to act morally, it is not necessarily the case. If it were, then those with advanced degrees would be more moral than those without.

Having said that, those who aspire to be authentic leaders should consider pursuing an education in order to develop the skill to reason morally at the highest levels. As little as one or two classes have been shown to increase moral reasoning ability. While a wide spectrum of classes in the liberal arts would be beneficial, specific classes would include any of those related to critical thinking or ethics. Ethics classes invariably consider ethical theories in view of particular case studies— "Would you lie to save your mother?" Most classes also consider a process by which a moral dilemma is resolved, a process that usually involves a moral decision making model.

To summarize, research has indicated that a direct correlation exists between education—particularly formal education on the post-secondary level—and the level of moral reasoning a person demonstrates. The higher the level of education, the higher the level of moral reasoning. Those with the highest levels of moral reasoning think critically with moral principles in mind, rather than either being self-serving or merely obeying rules. In addition, level of education is seen as the single most significant factor of influence in an individual's ability to reason. Those at the highest level of moral reasoning are guided by moral principles, including the virtues.

The role of moral reasoning is part of the authentic decision-making process a leader uses when addressing a moral dilemma in that it aids a leader in recognizing the moral dilemma and assessing the intensity of the moral issues. The decision making process also includes considering alternatives and establishing the intent to act authentically. The next section is a further discussion of alternatives and the intent to act authentically.

Decide Authentically

Not only do authentic leaders think with virtue in mind and at the highest moral levels, they also consider alternatives when deciding on a course of action related to a moral dilemma.

As noted earlier, the moral component of authentic leadership is grounded in virtue. What that means is that the leader is considering those alternatives according to those principles most consistent with virtue theory. The authentic leader is interested in addressing the dilemma in a way that not only satisfactorily resolves the issue, but results in the character development of the individuals, groups, or organizations involved. Of course, this is easier said than done, since character development implies a shared best vision for the individual or organization, and the best path to make the vision a reality.

Matters are not helped when virtues compete for a satisfactory resolution. What if a solution addresses the lack of humanity in a moral dilemma, but not the lack of wisdom? What if a proposed solution addresses ethical failures across all the virtues, but not as well as a solution that focuses in on only two or three? Virtue theory can provide some guidance in that the end goal of virtue is "the good life," such that an authentic leader can describe how a proposed solution is the best way that gets to "the good life"—upholds the organization's vision—for both the organization and individuals involved. Even then, virtue in-and-of-itself does not provide much by way of guidance or wisdom.

How do Consequences Influence Alternative Choices?

Besides virtues, one factor that influences an authentic leader's consideration of alternative solutions is the consequences of the alternatives. While the consequences shouldn't be the reason why an alternative is chosen—that would be using a teleological "ends justifies the means" principle—the authentic leader should anticipate the most likely consequences if a particular alternative is chosen. Other factors, such as obligations to stakeholders and organizational elements such as culture and resources may also help the leader identify an appropriate alternative.

The authentic leader brings his or her counsel, experience, and wisdom to the table when deliberating about alternative solutions, but it is no easy matter to identify and implement the best solution. The best solution may be fairly unpopular and difficult to put into place, challenging the leader's intention and resolve to act authentically.

Staying True to Self

Establishing the intent to act authentically is supported by the leader having a high level of self-awareness and a commitment to act in a manner consistent with "his or her true self."[10] Authentic leadership recognizes that virtuous behavior practiced by an individual is consistent with the individual's beliefs and self-identity, self-understanding, and self-concept—"Not only is this behavior consistent with what I believe, it is also consistent with who I am." The authentic leader sees him or herself as a moral agent capable of, and actually effecting, genuine moral change. The leader as moral agent displays forethought, intentionality, self-reactiveness, and self-reflectivity.[11] In addition, the moral agent is able to behave morally as well as resist behaving immorally.

Other research in developmental psychology is consistent with the authentic leadership idea that the leader's self-concept, or moral identity, rather than their moral knowledge is a better motivator for moral behavior.[12] The idea of moral identity acting as a motivator for moral behavior is best illustrated by comments like "Doing (or not doing)___is not something I would do," or "my mother did not raise me to be like that." The motivation behind the moral action is more directly linked with the moral identity of the individual than with what the individual knows to be right or wrong. The responsibility of a leader, then, is to develop a moral self-concept to the level of authenticity, which means embracing virtue, and initiating action based on that self-concept.

Staying True To Christ

While I am not a theologian, it seems the New Testament writers also use the concept of self-identity—in particular the believer's identity in Christ—as a basis for not only developing theology, but also as a basis for behavior (e.g., see Romans 6:4; I Corinthians 15:21 and 22; Galatians 2:20a; Hebrews 2:11). Since we have died with Christ, we are to live as Christ. The basis for a Christian life is not so much that Christians know right from wrong—although we do—it is that we have forged a new identity with Christ, and it is because of who we are that we live the way we do.

Act Authentically

Authentic leadership theory discusses how authenticity—translating thought into action—is connected with the moral self-concept of an individual. The more an individual acts in accordance with his or her moral self-concept, the more authentic he or she is. The last step an authentic leader practices after determining the best course of action to resolve an ethical dilemma is to implement a solution that is consistent with his or her moral self-concept. Implementing an unpopular solution requires the moral courage to withstand the pressure to do otherwise.

Examples of Moral Courage

Stories of moral courage are highlighted not only by the lessons they teach but by their relative rarity. You may recall the Milgram social psychology experiments of the 1960s designed to measure how far an individual would violate his or her conscience before disobeying an authority figure. One researcher discovered the individual who reported the My Lai Massacre of the Vietnam War also participated in the Milgram experiment, and in both instances showed a low regard for obeying authority figures in favor of following his conscience.[13] In authentic leadership language, the individual was being true to his self-concept and displayed moral courage when taking the actions he did.

Moral courage is the ability to carry out a solution to a dilemma in the face of opposition, whether the opposition comes from inside or outside the organization. A leader is authentic when the solution itself is based on the individual's self-concept and moral identity, which have their foundation in virtue theory. Moral courage bridges the gap between decision and action, and is more likely to be displayed if the leader thinks he or she can withstand the opposition, and whether the action is justified. An authentic leadership culture within an organization is more likely to encourage authentic behavior by an individual since the culture will not only minimize opposition to such behavior, but develop it.

According to authentic leadership theory, an individual's moral self-concept is integrated with the notion of an individual as a moral agent able to effect genuine change. The individual, as a moral agent, is guided by virtue theory in not only determining alternatives to a moral dilemma, but acting on them as well. Acting on an alternative is often done as a result of having moral courage, which enables the leader to act authentically. Authentic behavior is most easily sustained in an organizational environment which supports the leadership development of its members.

Summary

This chapter has attempted to develop how authentic leadership can address the moral development of those in leadership positions. The first step is for leaders to think with virtue in mind. Authentic leadership uses virtue theory, with the concepts of moral agency and character development of individuals, as a basis for authenticity. The second step is for leaders to think morally. It is possible for leaders to develop their moral reasoning ability to identify the nature and intensity of the moral issues. The third step is for leaders to think authentically, keeping in mind a decision-making process that identifies alternatives consistent with virtue theory and the individual's self-concept and personal beliefs. The fourth step is for individuals to act authentically, using moral courage to carry out an alternative consistent with the leader's self-concept and the character development of both the individual and organization. In this way, the authentic leader can both think and act in a virtuous manner, with moral courage, consistency, and personal integrity.

MY LEADERSHIP BOOKSHELF

Authentic Leadership Theory and Practice: Origins, Effects and Development, edited by William L. Gardner, Bruce J. Avolio, and Fred O. Walumbwa (Emerald Group Publishing, 2005).

Christian Reflections on The Leadership Challenge, edited by James M. Kouzes and Barry Z. Posner (John Wiley and Sons, 2004) provides a Christian perspective on their five practices (*Model the Way, Inspire a Share Vision, Challenge the Process, Enable Others to Act, and Encourage the Heart*

Lincoln on Leadership: Executive Strategies for Tough Times, by D.T. Phillips (Warner Books, 1992. A thought-provoking read, the book will challenge you to compare your own leadership style with a president who guided the country through one of the most significant crisis in its history.

Personal Reflections and Applications

1. The expression "honor among thieves" gets to the idea that even though thieves will steal from others, they won't steal among themselves. The idea represents the notion that there are some behaviors recognized as more virtuous than others. Virtues in this section were identified as wisdom, courage,

justice, temperance, humanity, and transcendence. Do you agree or disagree with this list? What virtues would you add?

2. *Street smarts* is an expression we often hear in relation to practical experience and overall "savvy." Do *street smarts* have limitations when it comes to the development of moral reasoning and moral decision making abilities, as compared with *book smarts*?

3. Think about the last time you were faced with a moral dilemma. Did you follow a moral decision model that considered any of the following: fact gathering; identification of the ethical dilemma, including various competing ethical claims; the ethical principles by which the case is decided; possible actions based on the principles, including which actions reflect the most relevant principles; and possible consequences of the actions?

4. What are some organizational obstacles authentic leaders have to overcome when implementing a solution to a moral dilemma? What are some personal obstacles?

Team Reflections and Applications

1. The story of Aaron Feuerstein rebuilding Malden Mills after it burned down in the mid-1990s is well documented.[14] In fact, it continues to unfold. While Feuerstein has never publicly claimed to be a proponent of authentic leadership, what authentic leadership qualities did he demonstrate when he decided to rebuild Malden Mills?

2.   Authentic leadership asserts that there are virtues uniformly recognizable across cultures. What does this mean for your organization? Is the sentiment of "what is moral for you is not necessarily moral for me" true, or can you identify a core set of virtues that you want to cultivate in your organization?

3.   What is the vision that drives your organization? How would you describe that vision in terms of virtues? How would you describe the underlying "character" of your organization and how it is embedded in the vision?

4.   Revisit a moral dilemma that your organization recently experienced. What could you have done differently that would have resulted in better alignment with your organization's vision? Or would have resulted in better character development of either the organization or workers?

5.   What does it mean to be a "moral agent"? How can you develop moral agency in those who work in your organization?

Endnotes

[1] See chapter 2, "Universal Virtues? – Lesson from History" in Character Strengths and Virtues: A Handbook and Classification by Christopher Peterson and Martin E. P. Seligman, 2004, APA, Washington, DC and Oxford University Press, New York, New York. Some may recognize Aristotle's classic list of wisdom, courage, justice, and temperance, while others may dispute his or any other list of virtues.

[2] Howard Behar, *It's Not About the Coffee*. New York: Penguin, 2006.

[3] Robert Goffee and Garreth Jones, Sept. 2000, "Why Should Anyone Be Led By You," *Harvard Business Review*, September 2000, electronic version: http://hbr.org/2000/09/why-should-anyone-be-led-by-you/ar/1.

[4] Tony Hsieh, *Delivering Happiness: A Path to Profits, Passion, and Purpose* (New York: Hachette Book Group, 2010).

[5] May, D.R., Hodges, T.D., Chan, A. Y. L., and Avolio, B. J. (2003). Developing the Moral Component of Authentic Leadership. *Organizational Dynamics*, 32 (3). 247 – 260. See Figure 1, "Developing the Moral Component of Authentic Leadership", p. 250.

[6] See for example, Kohlberg, L. (1980). "Stages of Moral Development as a Basis for Moral Education." In B. Munsey (Ed.), Moral development, moral education, and Kohlberg (pp. 15–100). Birmingham, AL: Religious Education Press.

[7] Rest, J. R., and Thoma, S. J. (1985). Relation of Moral Judgment Development to Formal Education [Electronic version]. *Developmental Psychology*, 21(4), 709-714. Rest is part of the Minnesota group, and his work generated the formation of the group.

[8] Walker, L. J. (2002). "The Model and the Measure: An Appraisal of the Minnesota Approach to Moral Development" [Electronic version]. *Journal of Moral Education*, 31(3), 353-367.

[9] McNeel, S. P. (1994). College Teaching and Student Moral Development. In J. R. Rest and D. Narváez (Eds.), *Moral development in the Professions: Psychology and Applied Ethics* (pp. 27–50). Hillsdale, NJ: Erlbaum.

[10] Hannah, S.T., Lester, P. B., and Vogelgesang, G.R. (2005). "Moral leadership: Explicating the Moral Component of Authentic Leadership" in Authentic Leadership Theory and Practice: Origins, Effects, and Development, Monographs in Leadership and Management, (3), pp. 43–81, Emerald.

[11] See "Moral Leadership: Explicating the Moral Component of Authentic Leadership" by Sean T. Hannah, Paul B. Lester and Gretchen R. Vogelgesang, in Authentic Leadership Theory and Practice: Origins, Effects and Development, Monographs in Leadership and Management, Volume 3, pp. 43-81, 2005, Elsevier.

[12] See for example, Bergman, R. (2002). Why Be Moral? A Conceptual Model From Developmental Psychology [Electronic version]. *Human Development, 45,* 104-124; and Colby, A. (2002). "Moral Understanding, Motivation, and Identity" [Electronic version]. *Human Development, 45,* 130-135.

[13] Kupperman, Joel. J. "The Indispensability of Character." *Philosophy*, 72, 2001, pp. 242 - 243.

[14] See for example, "The Mensch of Malden Mills", http://www.cbsnews.com/8301-18560_162-561656.html, accessed March 6, 2013.

Kurt Takamine, EdD
Chief Academic Officer/Vice President, Azusa
Pacific Online University

Dr. Kurt Takamine is the chief academic officer, vice-president of Academic Affairs and academic dean at Azusa Pacific Online University. He holds the rank of professor, and was the former interim dean of Business and Professional Studies at Brandman University (2008–2011), overseeing a 25 campus distributed system. Kurt has conducted consulting, training, and research ventures with Raytheon, Northrop-Grumman, IBM, Shell Oil, United States Postal Service, American Express, Capital One Financial Services, Microsoft, GE, and other Fortune 500 companies in leadership development, 360° assessment, and organizational change. His expertise is in curriculum design and assessment, instructional design, leadership development, multicultural and change leadership.

Dr. Takamine received the Distinguished Educator of the Year award from the Greenleaf Center for Servant-Leadership in March, 2006, the Outstanding Teacher Award for the School of Business and Professional Studies, Brandman University, 2011, the Outstanding Research Award from The Institute for Business and Finance Research, 2008 and the Distinguished Alumnus Award from Pepperdine University in 2013. Kurt was a Board of Trustees vice-chair for the Greenleaf Center for Servant-Leadership, 2008-2011, is currently a board member for the Engstrom Institute, and has written various peer-reviewed journal articles as well as two books: "Servant-Leadership in the Real World: Re-Capturing our Humanity in the Workplace" and "Why Good Churches Fizzle: Examining the Reasons Why Promising Churches Derail."

Takamine holds a BA in Social Ethics from the University of Southern California, Los Angeles; a BA in Biology and an MS in Environmental and Occupational Health from California State University, Northridge; an MA in Theology and Ethics from Azusa Pacific University; and an EdD from Pepperdine University in Organizational Leadership.

3

AUTHENTICITY AND TRANSPARENCY:
Is there ever such a thing as being
too open?
Kurt Takamine, EdD

A few years ago, I interviewed the top official in a major health agency, and asked him, "How much information do you share with your employees?" His response startled me: "You can't share anything of consequence to them. They can't be trusted, they'll use the information against you, and you don't ever want to expose yourself that way." In the years following that interview, I've asked other leaders in various sectors that same question, and they responded in like manner: employees cannot be trusted.

Employees are also hesitant to open up to their employers, because they fear the repercussions that might occur if they were completely honest. In one survey, 59 percent of employees stated that they would not share deleterious information with their supervisor until more than $1 million was in jeopardy, and 29 percent of those who responded would wait until the stakes rose to $10 million before putting their careers on the line.[1] Bosses that intimidate, chastise, or oppress their workforce will pay the penalty in lost revenue and profits. It isn't smart business to shoot the messenger.

What Are The Benefits to Transparency?

In a study by the Corporate Executive Board,[2] one key finding was that organizational cultures which promoted open communication and honesty outperformed competitors by more than 270 percent (in long-term shareholder return). Other research affirms that transparent authentic leaders positively impact the work performance of an organization.[3] There are four specific areas in which authentic leaders beneficially affect attitudes, which then translate into heightened levels of performance. We will briefly examine each one.

The Trust Factor

All healthy relationships are built on trust. When authentic leaders and followers identify with each other's needs, ambitions, personalities, desires, and even vulnerabilities—the relationship is deepened.[4] Authentic leaders are willing to display their shortcomings and mistakes with their followers, modeling openness and candor in the process.

What happens if the leader is uncomfortable or unwilling to display his or her weaknesses and mistakes in front of his or her people? Oftentimes you'll observe decreased productivity, increased turnover, customer attrition rates, and loss of revenue.[5] The greater tragedy, when leaders refuse to develop authentic relationships, is that emotional distress can permeate the organization, which creates insularity (or silos) within the institution.[6]

When leaders of an organization are less than honest with one another, when they put the needs of their departments or their careers ahead of the needs of the greater organization, when they are misaligned, confused, and inconsistent about what is important, they create real anguish for their people and the leaders experience that anguish themselves.

Jesus was the ultimate example of a leader willing to display his truest feelings, opinions, and values in front of his disciples, the public, and even the religious enemies of his day. Jesus invited the Twelve Disciples to shadow him everywhere, even though he was well aware that there was a traitor in his midst (Matthew 26:25). Jesus publicly defied social convention (John 4:9, 27; 5:37–47), confronted the religious leaders (John 3:10-12; 9:40–41), and displayed his emotions in front of others (John 11:33–37). Are we, as leaders, willing to be an "open book" with our people? Do our people trust us?

Connection to the Organization

Leaders who consistently live out their moral values, beliefs and convictions influence their followers to do the same, particularly when the leaders' behaviors are considered to be authentic. Recent research[7] has shown that followers are more committed to the organization when the leadership exhibits self-knowledge and self-consistency; that is, they have a sane estimate of who they are (Romans 12:3) and are steady in everything they do (Proverbs 4:26–27). You can count on these leaders to be unwavering in their vision, dedicated to the mission, and stalwart in their devotion to the organization's core values.

Herb Kelleher, former CEO of Southwest Airlines (SWA), exemplified the organizational values, beliefs, and convictions of his company. After the terrorist attacks of 9/11, many airlines struggled to regain market share, and several airlines filed for bankruptcy. SWA, on the other hand, has turned a profit for the past 35+ years, with a net income of $330 million; was ranked the number one airline brand by the Harris Poll; has been a multiple winner of *Fortune* magazine's *Most Admired Airline* and *Best Companies to Work For* awards, and has been recognized by *Chief Executive* magazine as one of the "Top 20 Companies for Leaders" 2002 to 2012.[8] The list of awards goes on and on. But, the thing that is so amazing about the Southwest Airlines story is the love, respect, freedom, and inspiration that permeates that company from the top down. Here is how the SWA mission statement puts this passion into words:

> We are committed to provide our Employees a stable work environment with equal opportunity for learning and personal growth. Creativity and innovation are encouraged for improving

the effectiveness of Southwest Airlines. Above all, Employees will be provided the same concern, respect, and caring attitude within the organization that they are expected to share externally with every Southwest Customer.[9]

Herb Kelleher sums it up in this way: "We have always felt that a company is stronger if it is bound by love rather than by fear."[10] Kelleher hires individuals that share the same values, beliefs, and attitudes of the executive team—including his own personal values—and this organizational commitment is infused within Southwest Airlines. In addition to the best customer service awards, and best places to work awards, SWA was awarded as one of the top 40 companies in the world to work for as a leader, which demonstrates that these organizational values start from the top and permeate the entire organization.[11] This transparency of organizational values fosters the commitments among Southwest Airlines employees.

Extra-Effort

The third finding from the research is that when authentic leaders and employees trust one another and are committed to organizational values, beliefs and convictions, they put forth an extra-effort in their work environment.[12] When positive attitudes impact performance outcomes, there is an opportunity to create high functioning teams.

Apple Inc. is known as being one of the premier high functioning organizations in the corporate world. Former CEO and Apple founder

Steve Jobs had a reputation for being demanding, a perfectionist, an autocratic and visionary.[13] As a result of his ability to inspire his employees to "go the extra mile," Apple Inc. has surpassed IBM, Microsoft, Dell, Android, Blackberry, and other computer and smart device manufacturers in sales and customer loyalty. Jobs' approach was to be brutally open and honest with his employees, even if he hurt the feelings of those employees that were emotionally sensitive. But he would also be fiercely loyal and appreciative of those team members that were competent, mission-driven and task-oriented. This type of transparency worked for the talent base of Apple, creating the extra-effort culture of this revolutionary company.

It might be argued that this type of confrontational, in-your-face transparency works in many high performing organizations, where one team member challenges another team member to perform at a higher level. You see this in sports franchises, certain corporations (remember the Jack Welch-run GE corporation?), and in elite special forces in the military. One could even make an argument that Jesus used this approach in his dealings with his disciples.

In various passages Jesus confronted his disciples, challenging them as Steve Jobs challenged his employees. In what seems like harsh rebukes, Jesus chastised the Twelve when they were fearful in a storm (Matthew 8:26), concerned about food provisions (Matthew 16:8), and with concerns in general (Luke 12:27-29). While we cannot know the intonation of Jesus' response to his disciples, we do know that he spoke the (derogatory?) words, "O ye of little faith." Jesus appears to be raising the level of expectation for his followers in their faith development, encouraging them to live out their faith in power and with God-given strength, so that they might change the world around them. These men—as well as the women that were part of Jesus' entourage—all became devoted followers in the faith when they were filled with the Holy Spirit (Hebrews 11; Acts 2: 42-47).

I need to clarify that I am not an advocate of in-your-face, adversarial leadership styles. I don't think that an autocratic boss can curry the favor of the troops over time, and prolonged chastisement can be counterproductive. However, the point here is that being an authentic leader does not mean that you are prohibited from confronting the status quo. A well timed, occasional challenge can bring out the extra-effort in one's workforce, if the challenged individuals are committed to the organization's values, beliefs, and convictions, and if the followers trust their leader.

Team Effectiveness

The previous three factors focus on the follower-to-leader aspects of authentic leadership (aka *individual-level outcomes*). The fourth factor centers on the leader's impact on team effectiveness (or *group-level outcomes*). How an authentic leader behaves (i.e., the way they communicate and interact with their followers), and how they are perceived (in relation to their character) impacts the team's perception of the leadership. One trust factor that affects group-level outcomes is called *vulnerability-based trust*.[14] Great teams are able to be brutally honest with themselves and with each other, leaving their ego and pride at the office door. How does one recognize when a group or an entire organization is truly transparent in this way? Here is how one author[15] describes this concept:

> This is what happens when members get to a point where they are completely comfortable being transparent, honest, and naked with one another, where they can say and genuinely mean things like "I screwed up," "I need help," "Your idea is better than mine," "I wish I could learn to do that as well as you do," and even, "I'm sorry"…It's ultimately about the practical goal of maximizing the performance of a group of people.

One tragic example of an absence of team effectiveness was noted in Malcolm Gladwell's book *Outliers: The Story of Success*.[16] In the 1990s, Korean Air had one of the worst safety records in the entire industry. One of the factors that contributed to the numerous crashes—seven catastrophic accidents between 1990–1999—was the hierarchical power dynamics among the Korean captain and cockpit crew. One aeronautical safety study affirmed this observation, noting that "captains often fail to listen and first officers often fail to speak."[17] In airline tragedies, the cockpit crew was often intimidated by the captain, and would not correct the pilot, even if the airplane was low on fuel, s/he was flying below a safe altitude, or there was a hazardous amount of ice collecting on the plane surface. These tragedies could have been easily avoided if there was a more equitable team dynamic in effect.

In the late 1990s, Korean Airlines hired Cho Yang-Ho to be chairperson of the beleaguered company.[18] He set up systems to prevent human error in the cockpit, and this correction almost single-handedly eliminated the crashes. This dysfunctional power differential was not just a situation faced by Korean pilots, but was recognized the world over.[19] Greater transparency in teams through vulnerability-based trust may have saved the air travel industry from additional pilot error disasters.

But is Greater Transparency *Always* a Good Thing?

Can a leader ever be *too* open? The answer, of course, is "Yes." There are times when sensitive information should not be shared in its entirety, particularly when the information is incomplete, unsanctioned, or premature. The information will eventually be shared, but it must be done at the right time in the right way.

There are times when it might be appropriate to provide the organization with a preview of upcoming events, such as the unveiling of a new product in the next year, impending layoffs, and even job relocation.[20] An example of the latter occurred in 2005, when Nissan decided to relocate its headquarters from Gardena, California, to Franklin, Tennessee.[21] Rumors began to surface that Nissan was considering a major relocation before there was any official announcement. To address any misinformation, Chief Executive Officer Carlos Ghosn, quickly notified his employees (by closed circuit TV and through handouts) that Nissan would make the move in six months. The employees in California were disheartened, while the people in Tennessee were ecstatic. Nissan's executives timed the communication correctly, eliminating any ambiguity through oral and written transmissions. The move eventually went smoothly, in large part because the leadership addressed the issue quickly and succinctly, squashing any rumors or misinformation. Nissan was able to remain transparent while timing the announcement appropriately.

It is critical to note that authentic leadership is not merely focused on candid and overt communication, but sees "their job as one in which they nurture followers' talents into strengths."[22] The next section will examine current leadership theories that demonstrate transparency in authentic leaders.

Maximizing the Talents of Your People

One unique aspect of the authentic leader is that s/he "recognizes follower's talents and sees their job as one in which they nurture

Authenticity and Transparency

followers' talents into strengths."[23] The authentic leader is not only aware of her own strengths, but she also feels the responsibility to empower and serve her people.[24]

This maximizing of talent is a common trait shared by other leadership approaches such as transformational leadership, servant-leadership, exemplary leadership, Strengths-Based Leadership, etc. (see *My Leadership Bookshelf*, below for more information on these different approaches). Empowering others for success, without abdicating authority, is critical for high functioning organizations.

When people trust the leadership, are committed to the organizational values, feel connected to one another, and are effective as team members, organizations become dynamic, organic entities. Work is no longer just a paycheck; it is a calling. Employees don't come to the job to punch a clock; they are part of a mission to change the world. It starts with the attitude, belief, and tenets of the leader, and goes viral from there, permeating throughout the entire company.

Seven Practical Takeaways

There has been a good deal of information communicated in this chapter, and it is sometimes difficult to distill this information down into usable, "bite-size" chunks. Here are seven practical application principles or takeaways for your company:

1. **Be transparent.** Keep everyone "in the loop." Let your people know both the good news and the bad news—they can handle it. In a strange way, they might even appreciate it, since they're intelligent enough to know when you're sugar-coating the truth. Your people want honest, reliable news, and they want to hear it from you.

2. **Be real.** Displaying your personal shortcomings and errors in judgment can engender trust among your team. Don't be afraid to be an "open book" in front of your people (as long as you afford your employees the same courtesy).

3. **Be unwavering in your vision, mission, and core values.** People are looking for leadership that they can believe in and rally behind. Be aware that you must not only "talk the talk" but you must "walk the walk." If given a choice, people will follow your actions, not your words.

4. **Love your people.** Respect, inspire, enjoy, and free up your team members. In being a genuine leader, you will also earn the right to speak into their lives, and it will make discipline and/or correction that much easier.

5. **Be honest.** If you are annoyed, upset, disappointed or concerned, your employees will perceive those feelings. Those are honest reactions. If you are pleased, appreciative, excited and motivated, your followers will be able to figure that out as well.

6. **Be respectful.** When being transparent always keep in mind that people will take to heart the words and attitudes that you exhibit. If you have to address someone's actions, that is

certainly within your purview. If you denigrate or humiliate an employee, that is never appropriate.

7. **Be a great listener.** Listening from the heart—that is, understanding a person's feelings *and* words—are so critical in bringing transparency into the relationship. We—as leaders—can sometimes fixate on the content of the message, not the emotional undertones of interaction. Experienced authentic leaders not only display honest emotion, they are also capable of regulating their emotion. This will open up the lines of trust.

Final Thoughts

Authentic leadership assumes that transparency must be conducted with wisdom, deftness, truthfulness, and sincerity. But transparency is more than a method; it is a reflection of character. A leader does not learn to be transparent; she develops into a transparent individual. An executive does not embrace "best practices" in becoming forth coming, but rather risks displaying mistakes or vulnerabilities because that is who he is. So an authentic leader is transparent both in disposition *and* behavior. Leaders that are transparent will foster greater team effectiveness, productivity, retention, and love among their people, which will give them a competitive edge over organizations that do not garner a high level of trust with their teams.

MY LEADERSHIP BOOKSHELF

Authentic Leadership Theory and Practice: Origins, Effects and Development, edited by William L. Gardner, Bruce J. Avolio, and Fred O. Walumbwa (Emerald Group Publishing, 2005) describes the research that undergirds the premise of authentic leadership. It is a little technical at times, but will provide in-depth explanations of such topics as humor, political skill, spiritual leadership, multicultural markers, and inauthentic leadership.

Christian Reflections on The Leadership Challenge, edited by James M. Kouzes and Barry Z. Posner (John Wiley and Sons, 2004) provides a Christian perspective on their five practices (*Model the Way, Inspire a Share Vision, Challenge the Process, Enable Others to Act, and Encourage the Heart*). For those readers who have yet to pick up *The Leadership Challenge,* this book will provide an executive summary version of these key elements. For those who have read Kouzes and Posner's work, you'll enjoy the perspectives of well-known pundits in the field of leadership studies, such as John Maxwell, Patrick Lencioni, Ken Blanchard, and others.

The Making of a Mentor: 9 Essential Characteristics of Influential Christian Leaders by Ted W. Engstrom and Ron Jenson (Authentic Media, 2005) provides clear, applicable insights into Christian leadership. Their chapter on *Honesty* alone is worth the publishing price of this book, as it explains what transparency is and what it is not, as well as the appropriate and inappropriateness of certain messages with direct reports. It is simple and comprehensive, and would be a good book for the team members or boards to read.

Personal Reflections and Applications

1. Mathew 5:37 (and James 5:12) encourages us to let our "Yes" be yes and our "No" be no. Are there times when you are more apt to shade the truth slightly, or to withhold critical information? Why do you think that's the case?

2. Think about the "who, what, when, where, why, and how" you communicate to others. Which of those components do you emphasize? For example, some people focus on the "what," while others focus on the "why." What is your focus?

3. How does culture impact transparency, if at all? For example, certain cultures might be very direct and open in their communication, while others are less direct and more veiled in their style. Think of some other cultures and imagine how you might be best understood by them.

4. Imagine when a trusted friend/pastor/leader has withheld important information from you. How did you feel? Why do you think you would feel that way? Why could have been done to alleviate some of your negative feelings?

5. If your leader approached you one day, and asked, "How could I create an atmosphere of trust, connection, and effort among our people, what would you say?

Team Reflections and Applications

1. As a team, share your best experience with a transparent leader, and (without naming names) your worst experience with a transparent leader. When are there times when over transparency is dysfunctional or inappropriate (if ever)?

2. Review the concept of *vulnerability-based trust*. Have you ever been on a team where everyone could be open, honest, and yet respectful? How was this safe environment created?

3. How might your team respond when faced with a public tragedy or crisis? Imagine that one of your products or services came under scrutiny because it presented a danger to your customers. How would you deal with this situation? How would transparency affect your plan?

4. In examining the four areas mentioned above (trust, connection, extra-effort, and team effectiveness), how would you evaluate your team with respect to effectiveness (on a scale of 1 to 5, where 1 = extremely ineffective and 5=extremely effective).How could you improve the lower scores?

5. As a group, discuss your views on transparency and how you might institutionalize these values into your organization. Rank order your values, and explain why you ordered them as you did. Then come to a group consensus as to the implementation of these transparency values, and how they will play out in your work place.

Endnotes

[1]Michael Griffin, "Open Door Policy, Closed Lip Reality (Part II)."

[2]Michael Griffin, "Open Door Policy, Closed Lip Reality."

[3]Hannes Leroy, Michael E. Palanski, and Tony Simons, "Authentic Leadership and Behavioral Integrity as Drivers of Follower Commitment and Performance."

[4]Fred O. Walumbwa, Fred Luthans, James B. Avey, and Adegoke Oke, "Authentically Leading Groups: The Mediating Role of Positivity and Trust."

[5]Patrick Lencioni, *The Advantage: Why Organizational Health Trumps Everything Else in Business*. Also, examine the article by Kurt Takamine and Baokim Coleman, "Strategies for Retaining Asian-Pacific Americans in the Technology Sector.

[6]Lencioni, ibid, 13.

[7]Claudia Peus, Jenny Sarah Wesche, Bernhard Streicher, Susanne Braun, and Dieter Frey, "Authentic Leadership: An Empirical Test of its Antecedents, Consequences, and Mediating Mechanisms."

[8] Southwest.com, "Fact Sheet."

[9] Southwest.com, "About Southwest."

[10]For a wonderful video explaining the Southwest Airlines philosophy, see the Charthouse.com *It's So Simple!* at https://www.charthouse.com/charthouse/product_film_soSimple.asp?

[11]Ibid, "Fact Sheet."

[12]Bruce J. Avolio, William L. Gardner, Fred O. Walumbwa, Fred Luthans, and Douglas R. May, "Unlocking the Mask: A Look at the Process by Which Authentic Leaders Impact Follower Attitudes and Behaviors;" Claudia Peus et al., ibid.

[13] American Public Media, "The Early Days of Steve Jobs and Apple."

[14]Lencioni, ibid.

[15]Ibid, 27-28.

[16]Matt Phillips, "Malcolm Gladwell on Culture, Cockpit Communication and Plane Crashes."

[17] Daniel M. Milanovich, James E. Driskell, R. J. Stout, and Eduardo Salas, "Status and Cockpit Dynamics: A Review and Empirical Study," 156.

[18] Roger Yu, "Korean Air Upgrades Service, Image."

[19] Milanovich et al., ibid.

[20] Karen Walker and Barbara Pagano, "Transparency: The Clear Path to Leadership Credibility."

[21] John O'Dell and Leslie Ernest, "Nissan Workers Lament Move."

[22] Larry W. Hughes, "Developing Transparent Relationships Through Humor in the Authentic Leader-Follower Relationship," p. 86.

[23] Ibid.

[24] Ibid.

Margaret Bailey, PhD
Vice Provost for Program Development,
Institutional Research and Accreditation, Point
Loma Nazarene University

Dr. Margaret Bailey is the vice provost for Program Development, Institutional Research and Accreditation at Point Loma Nazarene University in San Diego. Before joining Point Loma faculty she taught business at University of Southern California, University of California, Riverside, University of Redlands, and Loyal Marymount University. She was the founder and executive director of a strategic management leadership development consultancy serving many faith-based organizations. She earned her doctorate in business at the University of Southern California (1989) and MBA at the University of California, Berkeley (1981).

Dr. Bailey also worked as a financial analyst for the Southern California Edison Corporation and began her professional career as an officer in the U.S. Navy. While in the Navy she was assigned to the Commander-in-Chief of the U.S. Pacific Fleet as foreign liaison officer, on the personal staff of the Chief of Naval Operations, and subsequently was attached to the U.S. Senate as a military advisor. During Gulf War I she was recalled to duty with the Military Sealift Command in Yokohama, Japan, where she served in international shipping and logistics. Dr. Bailey has served as a consultant and/or board member for many for profit and non-profit organizations in the area of strategy, financial management and leadership.

SELF AWARENESS:
What are the benefits to
"knowing thyself?"
Margaret Bailey, PhD

If you want to learn something that will really help you, learn to see yourself as God sees you and not as you see yourself in the distorted mirror of your own self-importance. This is the greatest and most useful lesson we can learn: to know ourselves for what we truly are, to admit freely our weaknesses and failings, and to hold a humble opinion of ourselves because of them.

-Thomas A Kempis, The Imitation of Christ, 1441

"When the seventy-five members of the Stanford Graduate School of Business Advisory Council were asked to recommend the most important capability for leaders to develop, their answer was nearly unanimous: self-awareness."[1] Bill George in his book, *True North*, identifies the five key areas of "development as a leader: self-awareness at the center of your compass, and the four points, your values and principles, your motivations, your support team, and the integration of your life."[2] The authentic leader is rooted in honest and realistic analysis that demonstrates a trust and commitment to serve and empower others to succeed. The self-aware leader views his vocation as an expression of his talents and gifts in a way that gives back to God, family and community and not in a way that is self-promoting. For the authentic leader who is self-aware, his life is not compartmentalized into a personal-self, professional-self and spiritual-self; rather daily living is a fully integrated and harmonized whole leading to consistency and integrity in every aspect.

The authentic leader who is self-aware recognizes how his engagement in a situation will add or distract and how others will perceive his involvement. Therefore, he evaluates every context in terms of the ultimate objectives rather than an opportunity for personal affirmation and is willing to engage or stand aside based on what is best in the context rather than personal gain.

The authentic leader recognizes where their personal knowledge will inform or bias decisions and, where appropriate, admit weaknesses and seek additional expertise. They rely on their self-knowledge to evaluate and process information through the filters of their personal values, moral discernment, prior experience, strengths and weaknesses. "Authenticity consists of knowing what being true to oneself means (self-awareness) and expressing oneself truly (self-regulation)—with discrepancies between the two resulting in a feeling of inauthenticity."[3] A lack of congruence between self-awareness and self-regulation leads to cognitive dissonance for the authentic leader and moves them toward resolution.

Emotional intelligence and authentic leadership scholars identify self-awareness as central to effective leadership. Daniel Goleman in his work on emotional intelligence identifies the "components of emotional intelligence—self-awareness, self-regulation, motivation, empathy and social skill."[4] In the authentic leadership literature, "Self-awareness refers to demonstrating an understanding of how one derives and makes meaning of the world and how that meaning making process impacts the way one views himself or herself over time. It also refers to showing an understanding of one's strengths and weaknesses and the multifaceted nature of self, which includes gaining insight into the self through exposure to others, and being cognizant of one's impact on other people."[5]

True to Oneself

First, cultivate awareness. That means you have to work on being open to God's presence in your life, believing he's there and wanting to communicate with you. One way to do this is at the end of the day ask yourself how you feel spiritually about what's going on in your life. How you are reacting, at your core, to the circumstances of life?

Second, cultivate understanding. This comes through reflecting on your reactions. Ask God what feelings are from him and what feelings are not from him. In doing that, you will start to realize what makes you truly happy and truly sad. You will start to hear God's voice directing you through both your emotions and your reason.

Third, take action. Use your will to choose what God wants for you and reject what he does not want.
    –"The Spiritual Exercises," Saint Ignatius of Loyal[6]

The authentic leader who is solidly grounded in self-awareness will avoid missteps that can lure them into a situation that will violate their values, good judgment, or depend on skills or knowledge outside their own ability. As a young Navy officer, I served on the personal staff of the Chief of Naval Operations (CNO) James L. Holloway, III. A position on the CNO's high-profile staff is a gold star in any Navy officer's resume and many were clamoring for the opportunity. However, a high-flying career officer who excels in the operational fleet, too often flounders when it comes to the fishbowl experience of conducting tedious administrative duties required for the Pentagon. Few stay beyond a couple of years.

At the core of this simple example is the fact that many of these young Navy officers lacked self-awareness. They did not have the personal insight as to whether or not their skills as a fighter pilot or surface warfare officer were a good match with the highly politicized environment inside the D.C. Beltway and Pentagon staff. This same scenario is repeated many times in organizations as excellent managers are promoted up the corporate or ministry ladder to arrive at a position where the individual is a disruptive misfit. Laurence Peter and Raymond Hull captured this phenomenon in their 1969 book, *The Peter Principle*, where they identified the practice of companies promoting individuals based on their skills and performance to finally rise to a point that exceeds their abilities.

In his research on emotional intelligence, Daniel Goleman noted that individuals who are self-aware will not be lured by financial gain to take a position that is not a match with their strengths. Many years ago when I was on the faculty of a large private university there was an opening for the position of dean of the School of Business. I was convinced my friend, Mary, would be brilliant in the position. Each day I would make my case pleading with her to apply for the position and rescue us from a succession of awful leaders. After tolerating my antics for several days, Mary finally informed me, "It is not a question of whether or not I have the knowledge or skills to do the job—rather, the bottom line is the dean's job will not give me joy." This response revealed a deep self-awareness that comes from years of self-reflection and self-observation in different contexts. No matter how I made my case Mary was not going to be flattered into taking a job that did not fit with what she knew about herself.

Build on Strengths

Self-awareness is the opposite of self-love. Daniel Goleman defines self-awareness as, "having a deep understanding of one's emotions, as well as one's strengths and limitations and one's values and motives. People with strong self-awareness are realistic—neither overly self-critical nor naively hopeful. Rather, they are honest with themselves about themselves. And, they are honest about themselves with others, even to the point of being able to laugh at their own foibles."[7] He goes on to say that people who are self-aware have clear understanding of their core values and goals, demonstrate self-confidence, know their strengths and focus on what is best for the organization, avoiding self-serving decisions. Because they are confident in their own strengths they perceive how others may view them, they hold themselves in check rather than wandering into areas they do not belong or are weak.

The leader who builds strength-to-strength, models affirmative behavior that encourages others to imagine ways their own abilities may lead to greater gains for the organization. Leveraging the team's gifts and talents promotes confidence and recognizes each individual's unique contributions and interdependence. This in turn helps the organization to focus on its distinctive mission and avoids costly explorations into areas where there is a lack of mission-fit. Mission drift often occurs when individuals are seeking self-serving benefits at the expense of the organization. Mort Meyerson, chairman of Perot Systems said, that the primary task of being a leader is to make sure that the organization knows itself. That is, we must realize that our task is to call people together often, so that everyone gains clarity about whom we are, who we've just become, who we still want to be… Organizations that are clear at their core hold themselves together because of their deep congruence. People are then free to explore new avenues of activity, new ventures and customers, in ways that make sense for the organization."[8]

At the end of his earthly ministry, in Jesus' longest recorded prayer he reflects on his purpose, values, leadership successes, and his father's vision. "Father, the hour has come. Glorify your Son, that your Son may glorify you. For you granted him authority over all people that he might give eternal life to all those you have given him. Now this is eternal life: that they know you, the only true God, and Jesus Christ, whom you have sent. I have brought you glory on earth by finishing the work you gave me to do. And now, Father, glorify me in your presence with the glory I had with you before the world began" (John 17: 1b-5). Throughout his ministry, Jesus exemplified extraordinary self-awareness. He was never lured by flattery, he was laser-focused on the Father's mission, he understood his purpose and was not swayed by arguments to take the easier or more popular path, and he was never beaten down by criticism or elevated by praise. Jesus cared for and nurtured the people God had given him. He was deeply committed to their success and invested in them.

Acknowledge Weaknesses

The self-aware leader is deeply conscious of their strengths as well as their weaknesses and this in turn gives them freedom to act with authenticity, sincerity, integrity, and without false humility. Warren Bennis and Burt Nanus wrote, "Recognizing strengths and compensating for weaknesses represent the first step in achieving positive self-regard."[9] The self-aware leader realizes she does not need to be the smartest person in the room but will seek out people who can shore-up those areas where she is weak. They are comfortable with being challenged and encourage constructive debates and do not seek personal approval for conflict resolution. They are not threatened or jealous of others with greater knowledge or expertise but rather intentionally celebrate the accomplishments of others. They recognize the contributions of others, and are quick to give credit to deserving individuals. They are encouragers and at the same time view every undertaking as a synergy of gifts and talents.

Max De Pree, former chairman and CEO of Herman Miller, Inc. wrote in his book, *The Art of Leadership*, "Effective influencing and understanding spring largely from healthy relationship among the members of the group. Leaders need to foster environments and work processes within which people can develop high-quality relationships— relationships with each other, relationships with the group with which we work, relationships with our clients and customers."[10] He went on to write, "Leaders owe a certainty maturity. Maturity as expressed in a sense of self-worth, a sense of belonging, a sense of expectancy, a sense of responsibility, a sense of accountability, and a sense of equality."[11]

The self-aware leader is often self-deprecating in recognizing their weaknesses. Former chairman and CEO of Medtronic, Bill George, noted in his book, *Authentic Leadership*, "Only recently have I realized that my strengths and weaknesses are two sides of the same coin. By challenging others in business meetings, I am able to get quickly to the heart of the issues, but my approach unnerves and intimidates less confident people."[12] These leaders are able to focus on what matters and do not become distracted by personal criticism. In their research in authentic leadership, Adrian Chan, Sean Hannah and William Gardner propose, "By remaining true to self, authentic leaders experience less dysfunctional cognitive disequilibrium such as poor self-esteem, negative affect and hope, than would otherwise be felt from incongruent behaviors. Their consistent and transparent actions likewise elicit positive follower feedback that provides for self-verification and reinforcement of self."[13] These scholars also posited, "...that authenticity in leaders is an important leadership multiplier, and is foundational for producing virtuous cycle of performance and learning for leaders, followers, and organizations."[14]

Benefits to Self-Awareness

It is much safer for one's ego to be led than to lead and in this way one can avoid the painful discoveries that result in deeper levels of self-awareness. It is easier to live in denial than to invite feedback and easier to have confidence in one's own judgment than to seek the opinions of others, especially from those with whom we have experienced a difference of opinion. However, these self-protection mechanisms are limiting and will prevent us from both growing in our leadership abilities as well as limit our availability to be used by God.

Benefit one: *Self-reflection.* The time and effort committed to self-reflection and thoughtful analysis allows the leader to evaluate events in the context of their own values and motives as well as the organization's strategic priorities. "Self-aware people typically find time to reflect quietly, often off by themselves, which allows them to think things over rather than react impulsively. Many outstanding leaders, in fact, bring to their work life the thoughtful mode of self-reflection that they cultivate in their spiritual lives."[15] Industry rivals Bill Gates and Steve Jobs are both examples of individuals that set aside significant periods of time to get away for self-reflection.

For most of us the biggest hindrance to self-reflection is yielding to the urgency of the day and speed of communication that insists on instant decisions. However, self-awareness will only come through deep introspection as we are shaped through life experiences and the people in our path. "After he had dismissed them, he went up on a mountainside by himself to pray" (Matthew 14: 23). "Very early in the morning, while it was still dark, Jesus got up, left the house and went off to a solitary place, where he prayed" (Mark 1: 35).

Benefit two: *Self-knowledge.* "For I know the plans I have for you, declares the Lord, plans to prosper you and not to harm you, plans to give you hope and a future" (Jeremiah 29: 11). A leader is not authentic if she mimics Jesus; rather we are to be the image of Christ Jesus in the core of our character, values, and thoughts. This includes relating with him in His suffering. Yet, we take great effort to dodge crisis or avoid hardship that can become our greatest gain in self-awareness. Times of hardship often carve into our soul the deepest lessons that God has for us about our own strengths, weaknesses and most importantly dependence on Him. When I consider those events that most shaped my leadership they came through challenges where I was totally and painfully aware of my limitations and dependence on God's intervention and rescue.

In 1990 my Marine Corps husband was deployed to the Gulf War and I was recalled to active duty. This was at a time when our daughter was just five months old and would have to be left in the care of her elderly grandmother. The hours before my departure for duty in Yokohama, Japan, I wrestled with God throughout the night in prayer. Toward daybreak a deep sense of God's peace enveloped me and I knew that my little family was in His care. Even though I did not know the end of the story, and whether we would ever be together again as a family, I knew the Master and that was enough.

Thomas à Kempis describes the resolution of the life's challenges through God's intervention in this way:

> "Sometimes it is good for us to have troubles and hardships, for they often call us back to our own hearts. Once there, we know ourselves to be strangers in this world, and we know that we may not believe in anything that it has to offer…Indeed, we are sometimes better at seeking God when people have nothing but bad things to say about us and when they refuse to give us credit for the good things we have done! That being the case, we should root ourselves in God that we do not need to look for comfort anywhere else."[16]

Benefit three: *Feelings and emotions.* A leader's judgment is often overridden by emotions and feelings. A self-aware leader recognizes when feelings are involved and admits the challenges of working through the emotional context to an objective decision. It is much better to wait and allow the emotion to pass rather than speak and have to work through the damage done by our words. Things said during emotional turmoil can often cause more damage to the organization, team, or family's cohesiveness than any damage done by the original event.

Leaders who are self-aware recognize the inner motivations that are involved and can openly and honestly confess their personal need for restraint. I once chaired a board that experienced a difficult leadership transition. In looking back many individuals have confessed their disappointment in themselves and how easily and often they were swayed by their personal emotion rather than what was best for the organization. It is challenging for a leader to stay the course and sort through the hyperbole and criticism in order to focus on the mission and strategic priorities. However, the self-aware leader remains centered and focused knowing that once the wave of emotion passes relationship restoration can begin.

Benefit four: *Self-acceptance.* "Before I formed you in the womb I knew you, before you were born I dedicated you, a prophet to the nations I appointed you" (Jeremiah 1:5) Among the biggest blinders to self-awareness is denial. Too often our self-protective visors go up and we assume that it is others who have a problem and not us. Self-awareness begins with accepting yourself and all the flaws that come along with that knowledge. Cover-up is the first reflex of those who seek refuge in denial. These individuals maintain a pretense of authenticity. Former Medtronic CEO, Bill George writes, "Once armed with a high level of self-awareness and self-acceptance, it is much easier to regulate yourself and your feelings. Your anger and emotional outbursts usually result when someone penetrates to the core of what you do not like about yourself or still cannot accept. By accepting yourself just as you are, you are no longer vulnerable to these hurts and are prepared to interact authentically with others who come into your life—your family, friends, coworkers, even complete strangers."[17]

There is great freedom in releasing the disguise and accepting yourself in order to build on your strengths and pursue those goals that maximize your talent. Once I let go and admit (first to myself and then to others) my failings and flaws, I will probably find out that the only person I was fooling was me.

Benefit five: *Perspective*. The leader who is self-aware frequently pauses to ask the larger conceptual questions that help maintain the individual and organization's mission-centered focus. Why are we doing this and how does it add value to the mission? What is the value proposition for the customer or client? How does this action contribute to the strategic objectives? Who does this really serve? Is this approach sustainable and financially viable? The authentic leader, who frequently asks these questions of himself, finds it natural to ask these larger conceptual questions in the organizational context. These are questions that, if answered honestly, may yield surprising answers.

People who lack self-awareness are easily distracted and lose sight of the bigger picture. Authentic leaders have a compass that keeps them centered and avoids being distracted or pulled off mission. When embarking on new endeavors they will conduct their due diligence and seek multiple opinions before engaging in a course of action that could lead them or the organization off-track. They are not lured by headlines, quick returns, big gains, titles or prestige.

Benefit six: *Peace.* Busyness is the greatest obstacle to self-awareness for most of us who are in constant contact through email, smart phones, twitter, RSS feeds, text messaging, and on and on. Protecting time for self-reflection in order to gain perspective is antithetical to our daily routines. Even spending quality time in silence and devotions with God each day has to be vigilantly protected. But it is because of the demands on our schedule that we need to be intentional about our time to process, reflect and pray. The greatest insights we will have in how to resolve a conflict or undertake a challenge will come from periods of insightful reflection and prayer. And it is only through prayer that we will experience God's peace.

Final Thoughts

Leaders are shapers of organizational culture. The authentic leader is aware how his or her actions and attitudes impact the community. For the authentic leader, self-awareness is the critical starting point that begins the continuous cycle of experiencing, reflection, learning, and reforming the leader's self-knowledge. The more highly developed the authentic leader's self-awareness the more it leads to consistency, predictability, vulnerability, self-disclosure, integrity, transparency, and accountability

Authentic leadership emerges from our life experience and deep learning through reflection on experiences and what God is doing in and through us. Deep and lasting gains in self-awareness often come as the result of painful events, personal crisis, despair, and challenges that all of us try desperately to avoid. In Jesus journey to the cross, "He withdrew about a stone's throw beyond them, knelt down and prayed, 'Father, if you are willing, take this cup from me; yet not my will, but yours be done." (Luke 22: 41-42) These are events where God has shaped us through the fire and while we may never want to repeat the experience we understand how it formed us more in His image.

Former CEO of the OTF Group and co-founder of the philanthropic SEVEN Fund, Andreas Widmer in his book, *The Pope and the CEO*, recounts a time when he was serving in the Vatican Swiss Guard assigned to Pope John Paul II. An American priest was in Roman to attend a conference and he encountered a beggar on the street who looked familiar. When he questioned the beggar he learned they had been to seminary together but life events and bad choices had led the fallen priest to his current state.

The American priest was deeply moved and troubled by the beggar's life story and when given an opportunity for an audience with the Pope, he shared the beggar's story with Pope John Paul who in turn invited the priest to bring the beggar to dinner in the Vatican. That evening in their private dinner with the Pope, John Paul asked to meet privately with the beggar. On their way home from the Vatican the American priest implored the beggar to share what the Pope told him in their private meeting. "Well, as soon as you left the room, John Paul turned to me and said, 'Father, would you please hear my confession?' I said, 'Holy Father, I'm not a priest, I'm a beggar.' And the Pope responded, 'So am I, I am just a beggar.'"[18]

Practical Takeaways

1. Take time each day for self-reflection and quiet conversation with God about the lessons He wants you to cull from the day's experience. Allow Him to help you think through events and evaluate them in terms of Biblical truth and values. Avoid rushing decisions until you have clarity about God's will. It is better to wait and pray than rush and regret.

2. Leaders are out in front and for this reason they are targets. If you have thin skin then you will not last long in leadership. There will always be individuals who will not like your decisions or leadership and often they will be the most vocal. Confront, where it is appropriate but realize it is usually not personal, even though it may feel like it, and give it to God to sort out.

3. If you understand your own motivation then you are in a better position to understand what motivates those around you. Always give praise and recognition away and never horde it to yourself. Take care and protect the people who rely on you, even if to do so may be detrimental to your own well-being. Put their interests ahead of your own and they will take care of you. Create loyalty by being loyal.

4. Help others learn from their mistakes. Share your own journey and how mistakes have led you to deeper insight, wisdom and knowledge. Do not sweat over the little things; focus on people development and the big picture. Respect is the foundation for all good leadership. Do not do anything (i.e. teasing, poking fun at, deriding, criticizing, etc.) to your employees that would bring them down in the eyes of their peers.

5. Listen with intentionality and feedback. Repeat back to those who are communicating to you to make certain you both understand. Try to explore the speaker's context and history and understand that you are both processing information through your own history, values and lens.

6. Know your own learning style, and explain this to your colleagues. Let them know how to present information in a way that will capture your attention. Do you learn by reading, hearing, or visual (you need a picture)? Do you respond well to telephone calls, e-mail, writing, or meetings?

MY LEADERSHIP BOOKSHELF

True North: Discover your Authentic Leadership by Bill George with Peter Sims (Jossey-Bass, 2007) The authors conducted 125 first-person interviews with top leaders. Authentic Leadership Theory considers the personal self-processing and controls that leaders use that they recognize as key factors in their success. True North suggests a pathway to leadership success and demonstrates to the aspiring leader how to create their own Personal Leadership Development Plan centered on five key areas: 1) Knowing your authentic self, 2) Defining your values and leadership principles, 3) Understanding your motivations, 4) Building your support team, and 5) Staying grounded by integrating all aspects of your life.

Leadership is an Art, by Max DePree (Currency Book published by Doubleday, 2004) Leadership is an Art was first published in 1989 and was an immediate success. Max De Pree brings to his text decades of observations and self-awareness what makes a successful work environment. His book resonates with scholars, managers, politicians, teachers, pastors, and medical professionals as practical insight. De Pree looks at leadership as stewardship, stressing the importance of relationships, and creating a lasting value system within the organization and community.

Team of Rivals: The Political Genius of Abraham Lincoln, by Doris Kearns Goodwin (Simon and Shuster, 2005). Historian, Doris Kearns Goodwin, writes a compelling story about Abraham Lincoln's leadership style. He purposely selected his adversaries, William H. Seward, Salmon P. Chase, and Edward Bates to serve on his Cabinet.

Not only did Lincoln skillfully maneuver these men who disdained him onto his Cabinet but was able to forge a strong alliance that guided the nation through the most difficult time for this young nation. Lincoln's wisdom, self-deprecating humor, skillful leadership were all dedicated to the greater good of rescuing the nation

Leadership, James MacGregor Burns (Harper and Row Publishers, 1978). Historian James MacGregor Burns' text on Leadership was awarded the Pulitzer Prize and marked a new era in leadership theory and scholarship. Burns meticulous research into national leaders from all aspects of their life, introduced his pioneering work in the highly influential theory of "transformational and transactional leadership." In this influential work he posits that the best leaders are those who inspire others to come together toward the achievement of higher aims. He uses in-depth cases studies of Leadership is the classic text for anyone seeking to understand executive decision-making, the dynamics of influence, and moral leadership.

Personal Reflections and Applications

1. Think about the benefits of self-awareness and possible barriers you may have in gaining deeper insight. Do you allow time for self-reflection? Do you often feel pressured into making quick decisions? How does that make you feel? What do you do at those times of stress? When was the last time you spent time in reflection digging deep into an assessment of your decisions, values, and motives?

2. Complete a personal inventory of your strengths, "For you created my inmost being; you knit me together in my mother's womb. I praise you because I am fearfully and wonderfully made" (Psalms 139: 13-14). Think about your Spiritual gifts and the way God is using you to build-up the Body of Christ. How is God using you to encourage, support, and develop others?

3. Conduct an inventory of your weaknesses, "Search me, God, and know my anxious thoughts. See if there is any offensive way in me, and lead me in the way everlasting" (Psalms 139: 23-24). How transparent are you about your weakness? How do you communicate your weaknesses to others? Is this done in a way that invites them to support you and be a member of your team?

4. How does your knowledge about your own values impact your decision-making? How do you feel when you realize there is a discrepancy between being true to yourself (self-awareness) and the way you are expressing yourself to other (self-regulation)? How do you resolve this dissonance? Do you have an example where you had to deal with this inconsistency in your leadership?

5.   Imagine a time in your life when you went through a hardship. What did you learn about yourself through that experience? What did you learn about God? How has this knowledge made you a better leader? How can you take your self-knowledge and strengthen others.

Team Reflections and Applications

1.   Have the team reflect on those situations in their leadership experience where they had significant gains in self-awareness. Did these situations come about because of hardship, novel experiences, self-initiated reflection, etc. Ask team members to share how they pause for self-reflection.

2.   Ask team members how do they respond to a crisis. Give a recent example where a member of your professional or personal team made an avoidable mistake that cost and how did you handle this? Ask team members how they deal with their own mistakes that lead to poor decisions.

3.   Reflect on a period of time when God stretched you beyond your capacity to achieve a goal that far exceeded your expectations. What inner strength did you have to pull on? What did you learn about yourself? What did you learn about God? How did this affect your relationship with God? How did this impact your leadership? Is there a similar situation where you were able to motivate others to achieve significant accomplishments?

4.   Identify a time when you worked with an individual who lacked self-awareness. How did this impact you and others? How did it affect the organization, mission, strategic priorities or operations? Were you able to communicate directly with the individual to help them understand their lack of self-

awareness? Why is it so difficult for people who lack self-awareness to gain personal insight? What would you recommend to the team about confronting such an individual?

5. As a team review the benefits to self-awareness and discuss ways you hold yourself accountable? As you have matured in your leadership, identify ways your self-knowledge has informed your leadership? What advice do you give emerging leaders about gaining self-awareness and holding themselves accountable to feedback?

6. How do you keep criticism from weighing you down and internalizing? How do you balance what is helpful feedback from comments that should be ignored? How do you keep your focus on seeking God's approval rather than your colleagues? Was there a time in your leadership that you surrendered, "God's will be done?" even though you knew this might come at great personal cost? What did you learn?

Endnotes

[1] Bill George with Peter Sims, *True North: Discover your Authentic Leadership*, Jossey-Bass, Warren Bennis Book, 2007, p. 69.

[2] George, ibid, xxxiv.

[3] H.G. Lerner, *The Dance of Deception*, New York: Harper-Collins, 1993.

[4] Daniel Goleman, *"What makes a Leader Different?* Harvard Business Review, June 1996.

[5] M.H. Kernis, *Toward a Conceptualization of Optimal Self-Esteem.* Psychological Inquiry, 2003, 14: 1-26 and Fred Walumbwa, Bruce Avolio, William Gardner, Tara Wernsing, and Suzanne Peterson, *"Authentic Leadership: Development and Validation of a Theory-Based Measure"* (2008). Management Department Faculty Publications, Paper 24, page 95.

[6] Andreas Widmer, *The Pope and the CEO*, Emmaus Road Publishing, 2011, p. 31.

[7] Daniel Goleman, *Primal Leadership: Learning to Lead with Emotional Intelligence*, Harvard Business School Press, 2002, page 40.

[8] Margaret Wheatley, Good-Bye, "Command and Control," *Leader to Leader*, Jossey-Bass,1999, 156.

[9] Warren Bennis and Burt Nanus, Leaders: The Strategies for Taking Charge, Harper and Row Publishers, 1985, page 58.

[10] Max De Pree, *Leadership is an Art*, Dell Trade Paperback, 1989, p. 25.

[11] Max De Pree, ibid, p. 16.

[12] Bill George, *Authentic Leadership: Rediscovering the Secrets to Creating Lasting Value*, Jossey-Bass, 2003.

[13] Adrian Chan, Sean T. Hanna and William L. Gardner, "Veritable Authentic Leadership: Emergence, Functioning, and Impacts," *Authentic Leadership Theory and Practice: Origins, Effects and Development*, Emerald Group Press, 2005, p. 32.

[14] Adrian Chan, Sean T. Hanna and William L. Gardner, "Veritable Authentic Leadership: Emergence, Functioning, and Impacts," *Authentic Leadership Theory and Practice: Origins, Effects and Development*, Emerald Group Press, 2005, p. 3.

[15] Daniel Goleman, Richard Boyatzis, and Annie McKee, Primal Leadership, Harvard Business School Press, 2002, p. 40.

[16] Thomas A' Kempis, *Imitation of Christ*, Vintage Spiritual Classics, 1998, p. 40.

[17] George, ibid, p. 83.

[18] Widmer, ibid, p. 138.

Bibliography

Allison, Graham and Philip Zelikow. *Essence of Decision: Explaining The Cuban Missile Crisis*. New York: Addison-Wesley Educational Publishers, 1999.

American Public Media, "The Early Days of Steve Jobs and Apple," http://www.marketplace.org/topics/tech/jobs-legacy/early-days-steve-jobs-and-apple, accessed March 23, 2013.

Andersen, Hans C. "The Emperor's New Clothes." *The Complete Fairy Tales and Stories*. Garden City: NY, Doubleday, 1974.

Avolio, Bruce J., William L. Gardner, Fred O. Walumbwa, Fred Luthans, and Douglas R. May. "Unlocking the Mask: A Look at the Process by Which Authentic Leaders Impact Follower Attitudes and Behaviors," *The Leadership Quarterly* 15, no. 6, (2004).

Avolio, Bruce J., Fred Luthans and Fred O. Walumbwa. "Authentic Leadership: Theory-Building for Veritable Sustained Performance." *Working paper*. Gallup Leadership Institute, University of Nebraska-Lincoln, 2004.

Avolio, Bruce J. and Tara S. Wernsing. "Practicing Authentic Leadership. *Positive Psychology: Exploring the Best in People* edited by Shane J. Lopez. Westport: Praeger, 2008.

Bazerman, Max H. *Judgment in Managerial Decision Making*. Hoboken: John Wiley and Sons, 2006.

Bennis, Warren (1999). *Managing People is Like Herding Cats*. Provo: Executive Excellence Publishing, 2009.

Bennis, Warren and Burt Nanus. "Leaders: The Strategies for Taking Charge." New York: Harper and Row Publishers, 1985.

Bergman, Roger. "Why be Moral? A Conceptual Model from Developmental Psychology." *Human Development, 45*:104-124, 2002.

Beschloss, Michael. *Presidential Courage*. New York: Simon and Schuster, 2010.

Bowlby, John. *Attachment and Loss*. New York: Basic Books, 1980.

Brockner, Joel and Phyllis Siegel. Understanding The Interaction Between Procedural and Distributive Justice: The Role of Trust. *Trust in Organizations: Frontiers of Theory and Research*, edited by Roderick M. Kramer and Tom R. Tyler. Thousand Oaks: Sage Publications, 1996.

CBS News. "The Mensch of Malden Mills", http://www.cbsnews.com/8301-18560_162-561656.html, accessed March 6, 2013.

Chan, Adrian , Sean T. Hanna and William L. Gardner. "Veritable Authentic Leadership: Emergence, Functioning, and Impacts," *Authentic Leadership Theory and Practice: Origins, Effects and Development*. Bingley: Emerald Group Press, 2005.

Charthouse.com. *It's So Simple!* https://www.charthouse.com/charthouse/product_film_soSimple.asp?.

Colby, Anne. "Moral Understanding, Motivation, and Identity." *Human Development, 45*: 130-135, 2002.

De Pree, Max. "Leadership is an Art." New York: Dell Trade Paperback, 1989.

Dutton, Jane E and Robert E. Quinn (Eds.), *Positive organizational Scholarship: Foundations of a New Discipline*. San Francisco: Barrett-Koehler, 2003.

Esser, James K. and Joanne S. Lindoerfer. "Groupthink and the Space Shuttle Challenger Accident: Toward a Quantitative Case Analysis." *Journal of Behavioral Decision Making* 2, no. 3 (1989): 167-177.

Franz, Timothy M. *Group Dynamics and Team Interventions*. Chichester: Wiley-Blackwell, 2012.

Fraser, Malcom. "Leading Beyond Self: An Interpretive Biographical Case Study of Ethical and Integral Leadership." *Human and Organizational Development*. Santa Barbara: Fielding Graduate University, 2008.

Gardner, Howard. *Leading Minds: An Anatomy of Leadership*. New York: BasicBooks, 1995.

Gardner, William L., Bruce J. Avolio, et al. 2005. "Can You See The Real Me? A Self-Based Model Of Authentic Leader And Follower Development." *Leadership Quarterly* 16 (June 2005): 343-72, 365-66.

George, Bill. "Authentic Leadership: Rediscovering the Secrets to Creating Lasting Value." San Francisco: Jossey-Bass, 2003.

George, Bill with Peter Sims. *True North: Discover your Authentic Leadership*. San Francisco: Jossey-Bass, Warren Bennis, 2007.

Goffee, Robert and Garreth Jones. *Why Should Anyone Be Led by You? What it Takes to be an Authentic Leader*. Boston: Harvard Press, 2006.

Goffee, Robert and Garreth Jones. "Why Should Anyone Be Led By You?" *Harvard Business Review*, September 2000, electronic version: http://hbr.org/2000/09/why-should-anyone-be-led-by-you/ar/1.

Goleman, Daniel. *Primal Leadership: Learning to Lead with Emotional Intelligence*. Boston: Harvard Business School Press, 2002.

Goleman, Daniel. "What makes a Leader Different?" *Harvard Business Review*, June 1996.

Goleman, Daniel, Richard Boyatzis, and Annie McKee. *Primal Leadership*. Boston: Harvard Business School Press, 2002.

Goodwin, Doris K. *Team of Rivals*. New York: Simon and Schuster, 2006.

Griffin, Michael. "Open Door Policy, Closed Lip Reality." *CEB Blogs*. March 29, 2010. http://www.executiveboard.com/blogs/open-door-policy-closed-lip-reality/.

Griffin, Michael. "Open Door Policy, Closed Lip Reality (Part II)," *CEB Blogs*. April 20, 2010. http://www.executiveboard.com/blogs/open-door-policy-closed-lip-reality-part-ii/.

Halberstam, David. *The Children*. New York, Random House, 1998.

Hannah, Sean T., Paul B. Lester and Gretchen R. Vogelgesang. "Moral Leadership: Explicating the Moral Component of Authentic Leadership." *In Authentic Leadership Theory and Practice: Origins, Effects, And Development, Monographs In Leadership and Management*, 3: 43 – 81, Bingley: Emerald Group, 2005.

Hannes Leroy, Michael E. Palanski, and Tony Simons. "Authentic Leadership and Behavioral Integrity as Drivers of Follower Commitment and Performance." *Springer Science+Business Media*, 2011.

Hollen, Patricia J. (Adapted from). "Psychometric Properties of Two Instruments to Measure Quality Decision Making." *Research in Nursing and Health*, 17, no. 2 (1994), 137-148.

Hsieh, Tony. *Delivering Happiness: A Path to Profits, Passion, and Purpose*. New York: Hachette Book Group, 2010.

Hughes, Larry W. "Developing Transparent Relationships Through Humor in the Authentic Leader-Follower Relationship," *In Authentic Leadership Theory and Practice: Origins, Effects, And Development, Monographs In Leadership and Management*, 3: p. 86. Bingley: Emerald Group, 2005.

Ilies, Remus, Frederick P. Morgeson, Jennifer D. Nahrgang. "Authentic Leadership and Eudaemonic Well-Being: Understanding Leader-Follower Outcomes." *Leadership Quarterly* 16 (June 2005): 373-394, 376.

Janis, Irving L. *Groupthink: Psychological studies of policy decisions and fiascoes*. Boston: Houghton Mifflin, 1982.

Jones, Gareth R. and Jennifer M. George. "The Experience and Evolution of Trust: Implications for Cooperation and Teamwork." *Academy of Management Review* 23, no. 3 (1998): 531-546.

Kahneman, Daniel and Amos Tversky. "Psychology of Preferences." *Scientific American* 246: 161-173 (1982).

Kanfer, Ruth, John Sawyer, and Christopher Earley, et al. "Participation in Task Evaluation Procedures: The Effects of Influential Opinion Expression and Knowledge of Evaluation Criteria On Attitudes And Performance." *Social Justice Research* 1, no. 2: (1987) 235-249.

Kempis, Thomas À. "Imitation of Christ." New York: Vintage Spiritual Classics, 1998.

Kernis, M.H. "Toward a Conceptualization of Optimal Self-Esteem." *Psychological Inquiry* 14, (2003): 1-26.

Kohlberg, Lawrence. "Stages of Moral Development as a Basis for Moral Education." In *Moral Development, Moral Education,* edited by B. Munsey, 15-100. Birmingham: Religious Education Press, 1980.

Kupperman, Joel. J. "The Indispensability of Character." *Philosophy,* 72: 242 – 243, 2001.

Lencioni, Patrick. *The Advantage: Why Organizational Health Trumps Everything Else in Business.* San Francisco: Josey-Bass, 2012.

Lerner, H.G. *The Dance of Deception,* New York: Harper-Collins, 1993.

Lewicki, Roy J., Carolyn Wiethoff and Edward C. Tomlison. What Is
The Role Of Trust In Organizational Justice?" in the *Handbook Of
Organizational Justice*, edited by Jerald Greenberg and Jason A.
Colquitt, 247-270. Mahwah: Lawrence Erlbaum Associates 2005.

Lind, E. Allan and Tom R. Tyler. *The Social Psychology of Procedural Justice*.
New York: Plenum, 1988.

Little, Graham. *Strong Leadership: Thatcher, Reagan, and an Eminent Person*.
Melbourne: Oxford University Press, 1988.

Luthans, Fred. and Bruce J. Avolio. "Authentic Leadership
Development" in *Positive Organizational Scholarship* 2003, edited by
Kim. S. Cameron, Jane. E. Dutton and Robert E. Quinn. San
Francisco: Berrett-Koehler, 2003.

Maslow, Abraham. H. "Motivation and Personality." New York:
Harper, 1968.

May, Douglas R., Adrian Chan, et al. "Developing The Moral
Component Of Authentic Leadership." *Organizational Dynamics* 32
(2003): 247-260.

May, Douglas R., Timothy D. Hodges, Adrian L.Y. Chan, and Bruce J.
Avolio, (2003). "Developing The Moral Component of Authentic
Leadership." *Organizational Dynamics*, 32 (2003): 247– 260.

McNeel, Steven P. "College Teaching and Student Moral Development"
in *Moral Development in the Professions: Psychology and Applied Ethics*
edited by James R. Rest and Darcia Narváez, 27-50. Hillsdale:
Erlbaum, 1994.

Milanovich, Daniel M., James E. Driskell, Renee J. Stout, and Eduardo
    Salas. "Status and Cockpit Dynamics: A Review and Empirical
    Study," *Group Dynamics: Theory Research, and* Practice 2, no. 3. (1998):
    156.

Mishra, Aneil. K. and Karen E. Mishra. *Becoming a Trustworthy Leader:
    Psychology and Practice.* New York: Routledge, 2013.

O'Dell, John and Leslie Ernest. "Nissan Workers Lament Move." *Los
    Angeles Times*, June 15, 2003.
    http://articles.latimes.com/2005/nov/11/business/fi-nissan11.

Oyserman, Daphna. "Self-Concept and Identity" *Self and Social Identity*
    edited by Marilynn B. Brewer and Miles Hewstone. Malden, MA:
    Blackwell, 2004.

Peterson, Christopher and Martin E. P. Seligman. "Universal Virtues? –
    Lesson from History" in Character Strengths and Virtues: A
    Handbook and Classification." New York: Oxford University Press,
    2004.

Peus, Claudia, Jenny Sarah Wesche, Bernhard Streicher, Susanne Braun,
    and Dieter Frey. "Authentic Leadership: An Empirical Test of its
    Antecedents, Consequences, and Mediating Mechanisms." *Springer
    Science+Business Media*, 2011.

Phillips, Matt. "Malcolm Gladwell on Culture, Cockpit Communication
    and Plane Crashes." *The Wall Street Journal Blogs.* December 4, 2008.
    http://blogs.wsj.com/middleseat/2008/12/04/malcolm-gladwell-
    on-culture-cockpit-communication-and-plane-crashes/.

Plous, Scott. *The Psychology of Judgment and Decision Making.* New York: McGraw-Hill, 1993.

Rest, James R., and Stephen J. Thoma. "Relation of Moral Judgment Development to Formal Education." *Developmental Psychology*, 21, no. 4 (1985): 709-714.

Scholtes, Peter R. (Adapted from). *The Team Handbook: How to Use Teams to Improve Quality.* Madison: Joiner Associates, 1988.

Seligman, Martin E. P. *Learned Optimism.* New York: Pocket, 1998.

Simon, Herbert A. *Models of Man.* New York: Wiley, 1957.

Southwest.com. "About Southwest." 2013. https://www.southwest.com/html/about-southwest/?int=gfooter-about-customer-commitmentS&tab=5.

Southwest.com. "Fact Sheet." 2013. http://www.swamedia.com/channels/Corporate-Fact-Sheet/pages/corporate-fact-sheet.

Takamine, Kurt and Baokim Coleman. "Strategies for Retaining Asian-Pacific Americans in the Technology Sector." *SAM Advanced Management Journal* 77, no. 3 (Summer 2012).

Tyler, Tom. R. and Peter Degoey. Trust in Organizational Authorities: The Influence of Motive Attributions on Willingness To Accept Decisions. *Trust in Organizations: Frontiers of Theory and Research*, edited by Roderick M. Kramer and Tom R. Tyler. Thousand Oaks: Sage Publications, 1996.

Tyler, Tom R. and Steven L. Blader. *Cooperation in Groups: Procedural Justice, Social Identity, and Behavioral Engagement.* Philadelphia: Psychology Press, 2000.

Walker, Karen and Barbara Pagano. "Transparency: The Clear Path to Leadership Credibility." *The Linkage Leader.* http://www.linkageinc.com/thinking/linkageleader/Documents/ Karen_Walker_%20Barbara_Pagano_TRANSPARENCY_Is_the _Clear_Path_to_Leadership_Credibility_0105.pdf.

Walker, Lawrence J. "The Model and the Measure: An Appraisal of the Minnesota Approach to Moral Development." *Journal of Moral Education,* 31, no. 3 (2002): 353-367.

Walumbwa, Fred O., Bruce Avolio, William Gardner, Tara Wernsing, and Suzanne Peterson. "Authentic Leadership: Development and Validation of a Theory-Based Measure." Management Department Faculty Publications, Paper 24: 95, 2009.

Walumbwa, Fred O., Fred Luthans, James B. Avey, and Adegoke Oke. "Authentically Leading Groups: The Mediating Role of Positivity and Trust." *Journal of Organizational Behavior,* 32: 4-24, 2011.

Wheatley, Margaret. "Good-Bye, 'Command and Control' Leader to Leader." San Francisco: Jossey-Bass, 1999.

White Jr., Ronald C. *A. Lincoln: A Biography.* New York: Random House, 2009.

Widmer, Andreas. *The Pope and the CEO.* Steubenville: Emmaus Road Publishing, 2011.

Yu, Roger. "Korean Air Upgrades Service, Image." *USA Today*, August 26, 2009.http://usatoday30.usatoday.com/money/companies/management/profile/2009-08-23-travel-airlines-korea_N.htm.

Yukl, Gary. *Leadership in Organizations*. Upper Saddle River: Pearson, 2012.

Zerubavel, Eviatar. *The Elephant in the Room: Silence and Denial in Everyday Life*. New York: Oxford University Press, 2006.

19516527R00078

Made in the USA
Charleston, SC
29 May 2013